I0407242

POWER FAILURE

How Government Growth is Short Circuiting
the Power of The People

by

David E. Fritsche Th. D.

First Edition

Power Failure

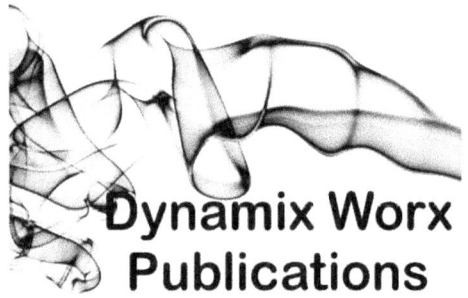

ISBN-13: 978-1470152543

ISBN-10: 1470152541

Dedication

To my editorial staff, without whom no one could read this stuff: Donna Krecklow, Alycia Partei, Jack Dunigan, Cary Craft, and the anchor for this book, **Judy McCollough**. My thanks, appreciation and envy of your language skills.

To those leaders I have followed in the past. They taught me well, either by their skill or by their failure - I learned from them all.

To my Dad. He was the ultimate leader -
- Some use heavy hands - Dad was light touch
- Some demand - Dad always suggested
- Some appeal to their position - Dad always built a relationship
- Some love the power - Dad always loved the people

William E. Fritsche

TABLE OF CONTENTS

We hear much about the **Left and the Right** - Conservative vs. Liberal. It is our paradigm - the matrix through which we view our political world. But Thomas Jefferson had an entirely different world view. He viewed politics through a different mind set - **Up and Down**! He saw power as resident at the bottom of the leadership pyramid, with the people. Government then, only had as much power as the people were willing to delegate upward. The power of government was held for the unified purpose of the protection of the people. The function of government was to act as the common mind for defense, while the people were free to use their own power to live their lives, conduct their daily affairs and pursue their own dreams and desires.

Something went wrong - terribly wrong. We have stepped back in time, past the American Revolution and the Declaration of Independence and our Constitution, to a governmental matrix where all the power is at the top and freedom is but a catch phrase. *Unless we regain our perspective of the direction that power should flow, we will be torn by the strife between right and left, and miss the more important issue of up and down.*

Power is not evil. In fact, it is an essential ingredient in the performance of the responsibilities of life. It is only evil when it exceeds the responsibilities that are legitimately given to us. Power, in and of itself, is not evil, but evil men will use it in order to achieve their illegitimate purposes of self aggrandizement.

All power is limited, just as all responsibility is limited, at least in the human world in which we live. Only God, the creator and endower of liberty to men, is all powerful. As mankind, from time to time, usurps the ultimate power reserved for God Himself, then, and only then, power becomes abuse.

I have studied this subject from an early age and have not found a clear and precise definition of power. It is usually presented as an evil thing, or as something to be desired in some pop psychological sense, enticing the reader to achieve it for personal status and gain. None of these treatments address the need for power within our given responsibilities to accomplish the task, and none clearly address the nature of true authority.

So, come with me and we shall go on a journey. We will walk through some stories of the past, look at some charts and graphs and we shall arrive, hopefully, at a clear and understandable view of power. The intent is that you, the reader, will be comfortable in handling the essential power required to accomplish your life's tasks while understanding how we, as a nation are in trouble because of the accumulation of power at the top of our political system.

Walk with me, and if you can, stand with me, as we understand why we are in crisis economically and spiritually in our land. Stand with me so that we may turn back to the foundations of our national principles, before it is too late.

We are a great nation, and God has blessed America, not because of our superior intellect or because we were arbitrarily selected for blessing. We have a blessed history because of the fertile foundations on which we were birthed. We may be experiencing the lifting of those blessings, not because of the arbitrariness of the One who blesses, but because we have forgotten the principles on which we stood in former days.

Come stand with me, and call our nation back to the place where blessings flow, where freedom rings and power resides in the place it was intended to be, with the freedoms given to the people.

The Author

Right, left and moderate are common political designations, which, for the most part, says very little about the content of one's political philosophy. Even our current group of presidential candidates seem to struggle to communicate what they believe at the very core of their political philosophy. Some try to communicate an image by identifying with Ronald Regan, but somehow seem lost when defining what that means.

The typical callers to conservative talk shows seem similarly lost with opinions that seem scattered across the philosophical landscape like weeds in a potentially orderly garden. What this all betrays is a lack of understanding of what is the essence of conservative thought. In the mean time, the Tea Party seems to be a target of pride and disdain depending on where one stands in the plethora of political competition.

So, what makes one a conservative? What central item of understanding underpins this ideology as opposed to any other? While we appeal to the positions of our Founding Father's we may forget that even they were not in agreement with how we should become a nation or what form that should take. In a very real sense it was left to Thomas Jefferson to define our foundations in the writing of the Constitution. It is here, in the mind of a man, that we find the power to argue his case and to carry the day in the confusion that was, our time of birthing as a nation.

Some argued for a monarchy, with George Washington as the first king. Others argued for a democracy, where the popular vote would determine our destiny. Some reached back to Plato and the Greek philosopher's view of utopia and the ultimate good for all men. The fight for a form was long and hard, but in the end, one central principle became the core value that is our founding principle: Power flows up, not down.

"We the people..." became the first phrase and the ultimate reality of a new nation. The reaction was against kings and tyrants, and the government that they constructed, because in all those prior systems, power flowed from the top down. All property belonged to the king or the government. All rights were given by the government and thus taken away at the will of the powers that be. The government was responsible to take care of the people because it held the power. That is the context of power and the assumption of government - power is held at the top and flows downward.

But Jefferson had been exposed to a paradigm shift in thinking that is one of the most important in human history. He believed and argued that power, property and rights belonged to the people and that government existed and served at the will of the people. The enumerated rights that are ascribed to the citizens of this new social experiment, he describes, were given by our creator God and no government has the right or any reason to enter into that arena. Thus our constitution is not primarily written for the people to set parameters for the living of their lives but is written to government to limit its intrusion into the private lives of the people.

The difficulty is in maintaining that perspective in the everyday administration of government. Politicians seem to seek power and accumulate it. The gamesmanship of the Hill, is the competitive need to pass more legislation, solve problems and garner the power to accomplish thing. But when the things accomplished rearranges the flow of power from upward in permission to lead, to downward in dictates of control, then we have lost our way and abandoned out roots.

This is the core distinctive of a conservative. It is a matter of direction. It is the desire to measure government by its response to the people and to hold it accountable for the trust given to it by the people. To move from this is the essence of political arrogance and the presumption of power brokers. The conservative mind set is seen in a willingness to allow people to live their lives, solve their own problems and to limit the involvement of government in how power is viewed. When it shifts to the top and is administered down to the people, it is counter to our system of government.

The conservative philosophy hinges on this one point: The direction of power - up or down. Depending on which direction it flows, we are blessed with freedom or cursed with control. It is as simple as that.

This book is about power. It is my desire that the reader will find in it, the wisdom to find the necessary power to function in life, but will avoid using it as a mean of controlling others. It is far better to lift others to the potential that is theirs than to demean them by control. It is also my desire that you, the reader, will not allow the government or other people to control your life in your pursuit of the beauty of what God intended for you to be.

The Author

Chapter One

Power Shift

The Winds of Change

One of the laws of science is that an object at rest tends to remain at rest whereas an object in motion tends to remain in motion, unless acted upon by another force. No principle is more true of the human condition than the fact that change does not happen in a vacuum. Human beings are creatures of habit and will, most often tend to repeat the same procedures and rituals as long as the result is acceptable.

Mind numbing routine does occasionally come to an end when the end result becomes painful and the desires of the person become unfulfilled resulting in frustration and a desire for change. It is at that point that we are most receptive to the phenomenon of revelation. Whether you call it revelation, a change of mind, a paradigm shift, or a peak experience, we have all experienced that point in time when we see something differently and our whole world changes.

This shift in thought process allows for scientific breakthrough, religious revelation and social progress. Nothing changes until a thought is planted and grows into an idea, which grows into an action. Change can be as personal as understanding that one needs to change jobs, or simply to turn the wrench the other way. But occasionally there are breakthrough ideas that seem to happen to a group or a nation or a culture. It is those times that alter history and allow mankind to move to a higher level thereby improving their condition.

For most of human history the government of groups of people was determined by the ascension of one strong person out of the tribe. The process may have been by common agreement or by bloody combat, but eventually someone became the ruler.

Most cultures and nations in history were ruled by the strong man or the system of enfranchised rulership from one strong man, down through their lineage. The rule of kings has been the most common form of leadership in human history. It has taken many forms, but it always follows the same precept: Someone has to be the leader. Someone has to step over the insecurities and fears of the common people and assert that they know what to do and where to go. Without this affirmation of power, chaos ensues and direction is lost.

Somewhere in time, about the 18th century, various nations in Europe began to ask, why do we need a king? For centuries, kings ruled over people and the experience was not always pleasant. The structures of social order assumed that kings ruled by divine right - that is, God ordained them and placed them in control. It therefore followed that if they were in their position by divine right, then they were not in power because they earned their position but because God gave them the right to rule and the position from which to rule.

Under this system of centralized power, there was no private property - all property belonged to the crown. There were no human rights - the king granted rights as he chose, or not. There was no vote - the people had no voice in the king's selection. The end result was a system in which finding favor with the king could yield certain favors, titles or position from which you could exact taxes for the king on a commission basis, or rule your own subordinate fiefdom with the king's permission. The whole system of lords, serfs, and subordinate structures of regal control were all related to the power of the king, and that power was total.

The French Revolution

In the latter part of the 18th Century, unrest gathered in France as the people began to feel the stifling effects of the monarchy.

The Estates-General (or States-General) of 1789 (French: *Les États-Généraux de 1789*) was the first meeting since 1614 of the French Estates-General, a general assembly representing the French estates of the realm: the nobility, the Church, and the common people. Summoned by King Louis XVI to propose solutions to his government's financial problems, the Estates-General sat for several weeks in May and June of 1789, but came to an impasse as the three Estates clashed over their respective powers. It was brought to an end when many members of the Third

Estate formed themselves into a National Assembly, marking the outbreak of the French Revolution.

On 13 June 1789, the Third Estate had arrived at a resolution to examine and settle in common the powers of the three orders, and invited to this common work those of the clergy and nobles. On 17 June, with the failure of efforts to reconcile the three Estates, the *Communes* completed their own process of verification and almost immediately voted a measure far more radical: they declared themselves redefined as the National Assembly, an assembly not of the Estates but of the People. They invited the other orders to join them, but made it clear that they intended to conduct the nation's affairs with or without them. As their numbers exceeded the combined numbers of the other Estates, they could dominate any combined assembly.

~ Wikipedia

The English Monarchy

The English Monarchy, at the time under George III, moved incrementally away from the absolute sovereignty of the King, with the influence of the Magna Carta giving increasing power and privilege to the common people. Following the loss of the American Colonies in 1776, the British Empire began a slow turn toward a constitutional monarchy, reducing the royalty to simple ritual roles and the reduction of power to figurehead status.

The Emergence of The United States

Parallel to the shifts of power structures in Europe, the United States became a nation state and established one of the primary documents in world history, defining a government of the people, by the people, and for the people. For the first time in human history, the basis of human rights was defined as rights given by God, and not subject to human control. Simultaneously, the power given to government was held to be a delegation from the people it governed, not a divine right. Thus a gigantic power shift in the structures of government was defined, in which power came from the people governed, not from God or the ruler or any other structure. Government was held to be by permission of the people and under their control. The whole thinking about government and its source of power, its extent of authority and its motivation for office was turned upside down.

With that shift of philosophy came a flood of changes. It was no longer the job of the government to control the people but it became the responsibility of the people to control their government. It was no longer the responsibility of the government to control the economy and to assure its success by central planning, but it became the responsibility of the private market place to assure its own success by the agreed upon exchange of goods and services by the willing buyer and willing seller. The scope of this power shift affected everything. The problem was, and is, understanding the scope of the application of this philosophical shift and of allowing it to work.

As time goes on, nations who affirm human rights and the power of the people, still tend to become embroiled in the task of restraining governmental usurpation of power and the controls of private enterprise, personal rights and the freedom of the people and their economy. The principle is that the vacuum of power, like any vacuum, tends to be filled by the existing mass that surrounds it. Government tends to grow proportional to the needs that are represented in the culture it serves. But if the power structure expands beyond its intended purpose, it creates dependence. In this exchange, we, the people, in effect, purchase care by giving away power to get it.

One of the foundational principles of Al-Anon is, when dealing with the addictive personality, if you support failure, you will get more failure. If you stop supporting failure and force the addictive and dependent personality to succeed or fail on their own initiative, or lack thereof, you provide support for success, even though the initial steps are difficult both on the person in need and the family that surrounds them. The track record of this principle is well documented. It works.

From the leader's perspective, to support failure by doing for others what they fail to do for themselves, is rewarding because you get power from them. This whole process is the basis for the erosion of the freedom we enjoy in exchange for benefits we receive from government. The vacuum, in this case, the needs that seem to have to be met, are either met by those in need rising up to meet their own need, pooling their resources with the community or family, or appeal to government to do it for us. When we give over responsibility to the government, it comes with the loss of personal freedom. The cost is measured not only by what it costs to meet the needs of those who require assistance, but also by government overhead which is always more than the cost of individual responsibility.

There are, of course, legitimate needs that can best be handled by government, but the point is to underscore the principle of the flow of power in the relationship of the people to the delegated representatives they elect to govern. In its purest form, government is limited to those areas of national protection and support that cannot be best done by the individual, community or family. Once the tipping of the pyramid of power begins and the people accept their loss of freedom in exchange, the inversion of the pyramid is certain and the people begin to serve the government which accumulates power and holds it.

History records the end result of that inversion of the power pyramid. It is seldom self -correcting, and unfortunately is seldom achieved by legislative reforms. Correcting the imbalance of power is usually messy, involving the overthrow of the government by the people. These periodic revolutions are the terrible consequences of illegitimate power being taken away from the people or yielded up by the people until they are ruled by tyrannical minutia, over -burdensome laws, and a government focused on fees to support its control of the people. In the end, laws designed to protect the freedoms of the people, become the means of stripping away those freedoms and of creating revenue for continued control and enforcement of the imbalance of power.

Seldom, in human history, has there been a true balance of power delegated upward and the limitation of the degree of that power. Inevitably, the existence of power at the top of the pyramid, tends to accumulate and expand, filling all vacuums and ends up becoming absolute power governing without the consent of the governed.

Chapter Two

Defining Power

According to the Dictionary: (Merriam - Webster)

1. a (1) : ability to act or produce an effect (2) : ability to get extra-base hits (3) : capacity for being acted upon or undergoing an effect

  b : legal or official authority, capacity, or right

2. a : possession of control, authority, or influence over others

  b : one having such power; *specifically* : a sovereign state

  c : a controlling group : <u>ESTABLISHMENT</u> — often used in the phrase *the powers that be*

  d : *archaic* : a force of armed men

  e : *chiefly dialect* : a large number or quantity

3 a : physical might

  b : mental or moral efficacy

  c : political control or influence

Author's Definitions

1. Power: The ability to accomplish the task; the enablement to fulfill the responsibility given.

2. Authority: Equal portions of power and responsibility. Having both the responsibility and the enablement to accomplish it.

3. Weakness: Having more responsibility than one is able to accomplish.

4. Abuse: Taking more power than is needed to accomplish the task.

Even our common dictionary definitions reflect the historic view of power, in part, affirming that control and power are thought of as synonymous. This ambivalence in defining power is also prevalent in those nations that affirm that power rests with the people and is delegated upward to their leaders. The problem is, if we cannot define power within a social structure, we will never see its abuse or the power vacuum that exists to be filled.

It was in 1962 that I had an experience that forever defined power for me. I have used this experience to define power, its need, use, and abuse in lectures to police academies for many years. The experience is as follows.

I was asked to come to the office of the Chief of Police in Colton, California in the Spring of 1962. I had taken all the tests to become a police officer for that department and was informed that I was on the hiring list. So, I dressed as appropriately as I knew how and reported to the Chief of Police. He informed me that I was being offered the job and if I accepted the offer, we would start the process of getting ready for work. Delightedly, I accepted and he told me where to get my uniforms, equipment, gun and when to report for work. Then he asked me to accompany him to the city court next door to be sworn in. The judge came out to meet us, asked me to raise my right hand, place my left hand on the Bible, and to repeat the oath of office after him. As we concluded the ceremony, the Chief handed me a badge and told me to keep it with me at all times and to wear it appropriately on my uniform. He shook my hand, welcomed me to the force and explained I was now a police officer in the State of California for the City of Colton.

I left the court and police department, got in my car and headed out to the uniform store to be measured and fitted. On my way, a fellow drove past me, going approximately 50 MPH in a 25 MPH zone. Being duly sworn, and feeling responsible, I sped up next to him, honked my horn, pointed downward with my thumb while showing him my badge. He signaled back at me, not with his thumb and not pointed downward, and drove off in a cloud of dust.

I was frustrated. Here was a person disobeying the law, and disrespecting a police officer. Something was wrong, and I was confused as to what had just happened. I thought about it long and hard all weekend, then, on Monday morning went to pick up my uniforms, duty belt, holster, gun, and equipment. I reported for duty at midnight as assigned, and rode off with my training officer for the night. Somewhere, through the course of the shift it occurred to me that I did not yet feel like a police officer. I had been sworn in and had been given the official stamp of approval as a police officer. I was as much of a police officer as I would ever be, in terms of responsibility, but I did not yet have the power to accomplish the task.

It was in that time of coming to grips with my responsibility as opposed to my ability, that a definition came to me. Authority is the combination of responsibility and the ability to perform the task necessitated by that responsibility. Power, in proportion to responsibility, is essential to have authority. If you do not have the ability to do the task, you are weak. Power is essential to the task.

I do not know if I ever encountered the fellow who gave me the finger and sped away again, but if I did, I expect I would have received a different response. Once I had the police car, the red lights, the siren, the radio and gun, I had the ability to affect his response. I not only had the responsibility but I had the power to go with it.

I have often illustrated this principle in police academy classes by coming into the class room after a break, as though rushed and announcing to the class that the prison, just down the street, had been taken over by a prisoner riot and they had overpowered the guards, taken all of their guns and they had called the academy for assistance. I then tell the class to go immediately to the prison and stop the riot. In all the years I used that exercise, no one moved. Then I would ask the class, "Why are you not obeying a lawful order of your instructor?" They would fumble around for a bit and then start giving excuses:

- No weapons
- No training
- No plan
- No given responsibility by the agency in question
- Etc...

Then I would come to their rescue and agree with them. They were all sworn officers from different agencies, and even if my giving to them the responsibility for the situation was legitimate, they did not have the ability (power) to affect a solution.

Responsibility without power creates weakness. Power beyond responsibility is abuse. You cannot ask your child to go mow the lawn if the lawn mower is broken. Many parents create weakness in their children by expecting them to do what they have not been given the power to accomplish. Conversely, many people in authority abuse their position by taking power beyond its intended use.

"Power tends to corrupt, and absolute power corrupts absolutely. Great men are almost always bad men."

This arose as a quotation by John Emerich Edward Dalberg Acton, first Baron of Acton (1834–1902). The historian and moralist, who was otherwise known simply as Lord Acton, expressed this opinion in a letter to Bishop Mandell Creighton in 1887.

One of the issues in leadership is the use of authority. If it is not used when needed then weakness is the result. No one wants to follow a weak leader. But the opposite extreme is as dangerous, and probably more prevalent. The use of power beyond the level of responsibility is abuse. It does not move toward abuse, nor does it become abuse over time. At the point it exceeds responsibility, it is abuse.

In our culture we tend to follow the loudest voice and vote for the most charismatic personality, without any concept of how they will handle power. Often, we ignorantly get the more forceful personality who is attracted to power and enamored by the power they pursue. In effect, we invite abuse by electing the one who seems strongest and who promises more to us. I have often said I want some politician, sometime, to stand and say, "I promise if elected, to go to Washington, go fishing, play golf and leave you alone to go about your lives and solve your own problems." This person might better serve the cause of freedom.

Yet, election after election we vote for the one who promises to provide more benefits, solve more problems and change things. So they go to the halls of government and, presuming that by the passing of laws they are protecting us and doing for us what needs to be done. Then, they proceed to incrementally refine the already millions of pages of laws and regulations to make even more. At some point, one would think that there are enough prohibitions, enough regulations, and enough pages of well meaning legislation, sitting on shelves of government bureaus, accomplishing absolutely nothing, other than the stripping of the people of their freedom, their initiative, and their souls.

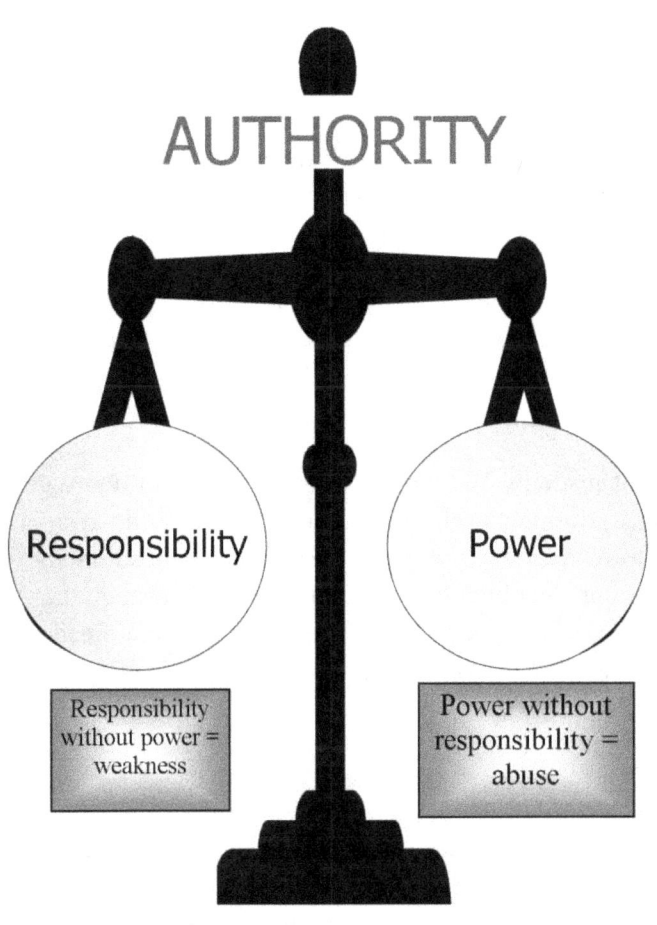

Chapter Three

Defining Governmental Responsibility

George Washington - *"Towards the preservation of your government, it is requisite, that you resist with care the spirit of innovation upon its principles. One method of assault may be in effect alterations which will impair the energy of the system and thus undermine what cannot be directly overthrown."*

"The powers not delegated to the United States by the Constitution, nor prohibited by it to the States, are reserved to the States respectively, or to the people" **Tenth Amendment**

This statement made by Washington was a warning to future generations of Americans, warning each generation that followed, away from the temptation to undermine the principles of the Constitution, the very foundation of our Republic. It is a warning to not exchange the slavery of governmental care for personal responsibility and the freedom of self direction. It was also a warning that, "alterations," on these principles would in effect change the fabric and meaning of the very laws established in the Constitution and as such the building blocks of our nation.

The vast size and scope of the Federal Government is one glaring instance in which the warning given by George Washington has been ignored. The Constitution does not specifically mention the "size," of the Federal Government, but it does specifically articulate the authority, responsibilities, and duties of the Government. The authority is limited in its scope and thus to its size.

The framers did not anticipate the tremendous growth this nation has experienced since its founding, but they did understand the nature of power and the tendency for those who have it to increase its breadth and scope and the need for limits. It is generally believed, by the people on the street, that the Constitution gives the government power while giving the people its rights and responsibilities. That is exactly backwards to the purpose of our founding fathers. Their shift from a top down philosophy of government to a bottom up philosophy of government, gave rise to a Constitution that acknowledges the power of the people and speaks specifically to government, limiting its usurpation of those powers. Each Branch of the Federal Government has specific Constitutional responsibilities that are outlined for that Branch. The Constitution limits government and recognizes the power of the people to rule over the government. Otherwise, our founding fathers, schooled in the monarchies of their day, would have given us a king.

Article I, Section 8 - Congress, (Legislative Branch), has power to: collect taxes, pay debts, borrow money, regulate commerce with foreign nations, establish rule of naturalization, coin money, provide punishment for counterfeiting, establish Post Offices, promote Science, constitute tribunals, punish piracy on the seas, declare war, raise and support armies and Navy and have exclusive legislative authority over the District of Columbia.

Article II, Section 2 - The President, (Executive Branch), Commander in Chief of the military, power to make treaties, nominate and appoint Ambassadors, public Ministers, Judges and all other offices, grant reprieves and pardons, recommend to Congress Measures necessary and expedient, convene or adjourn Congress, receive Ambassadors and other public Ministers, Commission all Officers of The United States and see that laws are faithfully executed.

Article III, Section 2 - The Courts, (Judicial Branch), power to extend to all cases of law arising under the Constitution and treaties, the trial of crimes and treason.

These are the specific powers granted to the Federal Government by the Constitution. Although simple in intent, keeping those powers from spilling over into every facet of public life seems untenable.

The argument is advanced, that since the founders of this nation did not know the future or the issues of the future, their power to speak to our future is limited. However, this creates a great dilemma. In opening the door to changing the Constitution in principle and reinterpreting it based on our perspective at any moment in history, we also open the door to the removal of the foundational principles on which it rests.

I used to argue with my students in my criminal justice class by asking about absolute values. Most of the students had already given up on the concept that, by its very nature, is an assumption of all humans at their most innocent state. Most cultures and most people assume there are some things that are always wrong. These are the given absolutes of the human family. But in the course of study, particularly in our modern culture, and within the setting of our modern academia, most students decide, at some point, that they were wrong and that all values are moral neutral, and that they are wrong because the general structure of our legal system, as a reflection of our culture, make them wrong.

So I would ask, "What makes an act by a given person, wrong?" They would all respond it was the law that made it wrong. Then I would ask, "So, if we changed the law to make it OK, is it then OK?" They would agree this is the case. So I would ask, "But what if we passed a law that murder, as we have defined it in this culture, is OK. Is it then OK?" They would always object at this point. The comeback was always the same, affirming that we would never do that. Our nation would never legalize murder. So I would ask, "WHY?" And they would answer, "Because it is wrong!"

At this point I would tell them, "So you do believe in absolute values and a universal code of conduct?" The conversation would then stop and I knew at this point their minds were open. They were trapped. I would ask if it is possible for the political process to become so vulnerable that people would be elected to office that were tainted with ideas and concepts that were, to some degree, evil? I would again ask, without waiting for an answer, if there was any historical evidence of leaders who had come to power who were evil and who murdered people either as defined enemies of the state in setting up a war, or internally within their own citizenry, as enemies of the state culturally or ethnically or.... They would then begin to recite instances in history where this had in fact occurred.

"What if," I would ask, "Charles Manson with his diabolical but commanding charismatic personality, were to rise through political ranks and be elected? What would happen to us?" By this time the class room was silent. Then I would affirm to the students, that for these reasons and many others, I did believe in moral absolutes, and I did believe in foundational principles that should underpin any social structure. I would also affirm that it was this belief, in our founding fathers, because they had seen the abuse of power and they understood the human propensity to garner power at the expense of human rights that our Constitution was not to be changed to accommodate the shift of power to governmental power brokers.

To the degree that power exceeds responsibility, it is abuse. It is not that it is tending to be abusive or could become abusive; it is that it is, at the point of its exceeding the limits of responsibility, abuse. Period! Pure and simple. We occasionally hear someone speak of the limits of power, but the basis of abuse is the limits of responsibility. When those limits are exceeded, the power that spills over is abuse by definition and effect.

It is for this reason that the framers of the Declaration of Independence included these words:

> We hold these truths to be self-evident, that all men are created equal, that they are endowed by their Creator with certain unalienable Rights, that among these are Life, Liberty and the pursuit of Happiness.--That to secure these rights, Governments are instituted among Men, deriving their just powers from the consent of the governed, --**That whenever any Form of Government becomes destructive of these ends, it is the Right of the People to alter or to abolish it, and to institute new Government, laying its foundation on such principles and organizing its powers in such form, as to them shall seem most likely to affect their Safety and Happiness.** *Prudence, indeed, will dictate that Governments long established should not be changed for light and transient causes; and accordingly all experience hath shewn, that mankind are more disposed to suffer, while evils are sufferable, than to right themselves by abolishing the forms to which they are accustomed.* **But when a long train of abuses and usurpations, pursuing invariably the same Object evinces a design to reduce them under absolute Despotism, it is their right, it is their duty, to throw off such Government, and to provide new Guards for their future security.**--Such has been the patient sufferance of these Colonies; and such is now the necessity which constrains them to alter their former Systems of Government. The history of the present King of Great Britain is a

history of repeated injuries and usurpations, all having in direct object the establishment of an absolute Tyranny over these States. To prove this, let Facts be submitted to a candid world.

It is in this phraseology that we see clearly the understanding and the intent of the Framers. They had been shaken from their lethargy by a paradigm of thinking. Their entire world view had been reshaped and they understood that power belonged to the people, and absent those guarantees, slavery would be the end result. Further, they stated clearly that the power of life itself belonged to the people, not to the government, and the people had the right, even the responsibility to reign in any government excesses in power.

The matter of where power is held was not a light thing to be considered. It was the essential pivot point of the foundation of our country and any deviation from it is destructive to the nation and the purpose for which it stands. While speaking to the limits of government, the founders also spoke to the power of the people and of their responsibility to not allow for those abuses and the overstepping of responsibility, which is common to people who seek power.

It is for that purpose the framers provided that the powers enumerated in the Constitution be the only powers to be exercised by the federal government, and that those things not specifically given as a responsibility should be reserved to the states and to the people.

Chapter Four

The Basis of Authority

From an article in Newsweek, Oct. 25th, 2010, Andrew Romano writes:

The Founders' masterpiece, O'Donnell (Christine O'Donnell) said, isn't just a legal document; it's a "covenant" based on "divine principles." For decades, she continued, the agents of "anti-Americanism" who dominate "the D.C. cocktail crowd" have disrespected the hallowed document. But now, finally, in the "darker days" of the Obama administration, "the Constitution is making a comeback."

From a legal perspective, there's a case to be made that O'Donnell's argument is inaccurate. The Constitution is a relentlessly secular document that never once mentions God or Jesus. And nothing in recent jurisprudence suggests that the past few decades of governing have been any less constitutional than the decades that preceded them. But the Tea Party's language isn't legal, and neither is its logic. It's moral: right vs. wrong. What O'Donnell & Co. are really talking about is culture war.

In this article, Romano accurately describes the contrasts, although also clearly revealing his anti-conservative bias. And, he is almost right in asserting that the Constitution does not mention God or Jesus. But taken as a whole, the documents on which this nation is founded do refer to the existence of God rather directly.

The problem is with our Constitution and the Bill of Rights which affirms that we are endowed by 'our Creator' (direct reference to a higher power) with certain unalienable rights. The reason for this premise is because of the history behind our founding fathers. They were breaking away from the historic governmental system of monarchies which held the premise that all power and all rights were in the king and the king could do no wrong. The foundations of this nation were to prohibit government from intruding into the private lives and private property of the people. So, we affirm that those rights are not conveyed by the government but by God Himself and that no government has the right to enter that territory.

So the lines of authority are: From God (the ultimate authority) to the individuals (people) and from the people to the government. That Romano affirms the Constitution is 'a relentlessly secular document' is to contrast religion with politics in a way that is exclusionary. I would agree that the Constitution was created by people. People create government. But the premise of the people creating this government was that they had freedoms from above that were not given by government and could not be taken away by government. To deny this one central foundational premise is to throw the entire national premise into the fire of power struggles and see who can accumulate more than the other in a race to become the next king.

In other words, if people hold the power of government under God, and have rights given by God which government cannot address nor take away, then they can construct a Constitution and a government to their liking and restrict the power of that government. But if there is no God and the documents are 'a relentlessly secular document' then the secular authority of our governmental officials is sufficient to rewrite it or ignore it as they see fit. No, I did not say that you have to believe in God to be an American, but you do have to accept the fact that it is based on the assumption of an all powerful deity who has delegated power to the people as opposed to the structures of an all powerful government.

So, if a person affirms that there is no God, and that He has not given responsibility to the people then they are at cross purposes with the premise of our founding documents and are predisposed to believe that our rights, although attributed to God, are really just flowery language from some demented concepts of our founding fathers and are not really true. So, they must conclude, absent a God who granted them, that they are in fact, given by government, even though it does not say so, and thus are subject to government changing its mind. This all relates to our concept of the Constitution and our founding documents. If the Constitution is a living document and subject to change, then so are our rights to personal space and personal property. We can thus change the documents and the rights they protect. Many, possibly most of our governmental officials today, seem to believe that it can and should be changed.

Against that position are those like myself who are strict constitutionalists, who believe those guarantees in our founding documents restrict the power of government and should remain as written. This restricts the courts or legislators from making legislation beyond the limits of the power in the constitution and focuses their power on reviewing law and public actions in the light of the Constitution - plus nothing.

Most religions in our nation, accept that we exist in two kingdoms, the Kingdom of God and the Kingdom of Man. In this separation of powers and arena of influence, both exist on a compatible and parallel track. It is in recognition of the two kingdoms that our founding fathers provided for the separation of powers, not only in the halls of government but in the right to the freedom of religion. Note: It is not freedom from religion, but the freedom of religion. Rightly understood, there is no conflict. Thus those who serve in government are free to enter the halls of the church without conflict and participate in their faith without threat to the government. Similarly, people of faith have the right to enter the halls of government and to serve or, petition, or influence without provoking a conflict. The separation of powers, or the acknowledgment of the two kingdoms, the state and the church, is the essential premise to the function of both kingdoms and the guarantee that our rights shall not be infringed.

At the same time, the framers of our Constitution did not want America to become a theocracy. They did not believe in a theocratic state. To allow religion to dictate the government is to remove the power from the individual persons of the nation, and is, again, to remove the philosophy of power as being held by the people. So the Constitution does not make place for the influence of the church, but reserves that power to the people. Amazingly, the revolution of the concept of how power should flow, included all institutions, together with the church and more specifically the limited power of government.

It is well documented that our founding fathers were religious men, mostly of the Christian faith. But they had experienced both the tyranny of the king and the tyranny of the church. They were attempting to right a wrong and to pass that structure down to the generations to come. People had the power and the responsibility. It was a focused work of the individual to hold property, possessions, and the control of government. The Constitution was never intended to limit the influence of religion on the individual or to strip the culture of the concept of God. It was simply constructed to exclude the responsibility and rights of the people from being accumulated in corporate bastions of power, whether it be the church or the state.

The problem is not that religious people participate in the kingdom of our nation, but that many anti-religious people do not accept the general construct of the Constitution, that the government or any cumulative power base within government or aside from government, cannot usurp the rights given specifically to the individuals within this great nation. Power does not rest at the top, but at the bottom. Whether the individual is Christian, Jew, Muslim, Atheist, or any other, the same premise exists: Each has responsibility for their own lives and the power to accomplish that responsibility. Each can participate freely in their own faith and in the delegating of responsibilities and powers to government, but none has the right to mess with the assumed fact that the Creator gave His power and responsibility to people - all of them.

Chapter Five

Choosing Our Level of Control

I loved teaching my classes in Criminal Justice. It was a creative context for student and teacher alike. One of the things I loved to do was announce to the class, usually early on in the semester, "crime is a solvable problem!"

That announcement would always provoke an argument from the class, which I encouraged and welcomed. Someone would inevitably argue, "No it is not. We will always have crime." Most of the class would agree. Then I would ask, "If there are any nations on the planet or in history who have not had as high a crime rate as ours, or are there nations that have a higher crime rate than ours?" The answers were usually accurate and in the affirmative. Yes there are nations with less crime than ours and those with more.

The follow-up question is, why? The answer is because some nations do not have any controls over the activities of their citizens and anarchy rules on their streets. Although all nations presumably have laws, some enforce them with greater or lesser vigor than do we. Some have an authoritarian system of control in which the police exact justice on the spot, by cutting off a hand or a head depending of the severity of the crime.

The fact is, the United States has decided on a system of justice that is more humane and exacting than almost any in history. We have decided it is better for many to go free than for one innocent person to be convicted. We have decided on a presumption of innocence and a trial by our peers. Our whole system is a choice between the degree of control and the resulting degree of crime. I argue that we could stop crime to a large degree by placing a policeman on every corner, in every house and by giving them the power to exact a penalty then and there. This is of course assuming that we could find policemen from a source other than the human race.

In the end, the class would agree and off we would go on a journey through criminal law, exploring the limits and guarantees of freedom inherent in it. We would explore the development of the law, the purpose of the law and the powers of enforcement. I enjoyed the class and the interaction with the students, but alas, I fear that we may have moved away from the fundamental assumptions of law in our nation. I fear that we the people have not guarded our liberties as closely as we should.

It is inevitable and right that we should delegate to our government the power to make laws to protect the general public. We would all agree that we should outlaw murder, rape, theft, kidnapping, child abuse, and so forth. We assent to that delegation of power and responsibility for the good of all. However, the subtle power shift inevitably takes place when those who legislate presume they know better than those who have given them the power. The motivation for legislation being no longer how to better serve the people and provide for their safety, but how to control them in general.

The mindset of many ruling politicians lacks any realization that they are to be serving those in power -- the people. This mindset results in the presumption they are an elite ruling class of people, destined by some reason or right, to rule.

> John Dingell (D-MI) made some incredible admissions on WJR 760AM, a local Michigan station, on Tuesday morning, March 24th, 2010, in response to a question from local radio host Paul W. Smith. Smith asked, starting at about the 6:00 point on the tape, if the leftist rhetoric is correct that tens of thousands of Americans die per year because of a lack of health insurance, "are we ready to let 72,000 more people die" between now and the implementation of Obamacare in 2014. Dingell then shockingly responded as follows:

>> *"We're not ready to be doing it. But let me remind you, this has been going on for years. We are bringing it to a halt. The harsh fact of the matter is when you're going to pass legislation that will cover 300 [million] American people in different ways it takes a long time to do the necessary administrative steps that have to be taken to put the legislation together to control the people."*

That is but one slip of the lip that betrays a problem that exists in today's political structures. The problem is the leaders do not understand and thus do not believe the foundational concepts of this republic. They believe, sincerely believe, that they are the power and that they are subservient to no one. They have to control the people.

The argument is often advanced by those who deal in making laws that this one more act of control is essential to public safety or harmony and that this is not a conspiracy of control. But those who experience the annual process of building more social constraints feel the effects of not just more constraint and the loss of freedom but of the cost of making the laws, enforcing the laws, punishing the people who have violated them and the whole culture of criminal justice.

It does not have to be an organized conspiracy to control; it is simply the end result of movement along the continuum. It is a slippery slope, as any activity for the sake of increased freedom or increased control moves the balance point along the line. There are no inconsequential actions that have no effect when dealing with this continuum. For each action on the line, there is an equal and opposite reaction, moving the balance point. Maybe we could call this the physics of social action.

There are many evils in the human family. People are seldom in agreement as to what is right, sensible, and moral or of value. We all probably laugh regularly at the stupidity of some human behavior we hear about or see on TV. The human race is a plethora of incidents that betray ignorance, stupidity or just plain meanness. There is no end to the imagination of the genius or the ignorant.

Once we decide we should do something about it, however, we have to understand the consequences of the inevitable effects our regulations have on the freedom of others. Law not only has consequences to the evil doer, but also to those who are caught in the letter of the law without having been the target of the law. There are always unintended consequences. The greatest of these is that the whole of our culture loses freedom in the decision to bring greater control.

You cannot do one without the other. The growing philosophy of government in many areas is that all activities need to be categorized and either permitted by government or regulated with some sort of licensure or prohibited. For government to be absent from any arena of life seems inexcusable to those with this mindset. But it is precisely this mindset that moves our society along that continuum of freedom and control toward the tyranny of control. Whether it is intended or not, it is an interactive balance that moves with each act of legislation. Good people with seemingly noble motives can exact control as well as the evil despot.

One of my personal experiences was with a Washoe County, Nevada official who was proposing a dog control ordinance. He invited various people from the dog loving community to gather at his conference room to discuss what ordinance would cover the perceived problem. Various people began to rise to the question and give input as to what the ordinance should read. I sat silently for some time and finally the fellow asked if I had any input. He shouldn't have.

I explained that he had set up the meeting to create legislation and all the input so far was in support of his premise that legislation was warranted. My lack of any input to the process was not because I disagreed with the individuals participating but with the assumed premise. "What if," I asked, "we just allowed the people to take care of their own dogs and make those individual decisions without the government telling them what to do or not do? What if we assumed that the people have both the responsibility and the knowledge to take care of themselves as they have done for thousands of years? What if the government just stayed out of this?" The other people gathered at the meeting began to look at each other and nod their heads.

The leader just looked at me dumbfounded and said, "But this is one of the items that the state has mandated that we address at the county level, since it is uncovered in our ordinances." I responded, "I did not give the state the right to mandate anything of this nature and I am one of the people. I have the power, not the state." He stammered, and did not know how to respond, but the people he had invited knew very well what I was saying. I left the meeting and he lost his support, who had now become part of a resistance to the ordinance rather than participants in forming it.

Until the people take their place of authority over government, our current situation will not change. We will be, in the minds of our leaders, the ignorant masses who cannot negotiate life without government control.

We need to be far more involved in and careful of who and what we give over to government of our right to self determination. Life and freedom are a precious gift given to us by our Creator. We should never give that away easily nor allow anyone to take it from us.

From the words of Patrick Henry, March 23, 1775:

"It is in vain, sir, to extenuate the matter. Gentlemen may cry, Peace, Peace — but there is no peace. The war is actually begun! The next gale that sweeps from the north will bring to our ears the clash of resounding arms! Our brethren are already in the field! Why stand we here idle? What is it that gentlemen wish? What would they have? Is life so dear, or peace so sweet, as to be purchased at the price of chains and slavery? Forbid it, Almighty God! I know not what course others may take; but as for me, give me liberty or give me death!"

Our founding fathers understood the continuum between freedom and slavery, human rights and control. If we are to survive as a nation we had better re-learn that foundational truth!

Chapter Six

Leadership and Control

Servant Leadership

Many years ago now, Robert Greenleaf wrote a wonderful book entitled, 'Servant Leadership.' It cut across all of the more popular books. You know the kind: Leadership by Attila the Hun, How to Get What You Want From People, Wrestling People Into Submission, How to Build a Forceful Personality, etc. Greenleaf proposed a repositioning of the leader by inverting the pyramid of the organizational chart.

Position is everything in dealing with people, particularly those who oppose us. Our world is oriented to the face-to-face power struggle in which the strongest wins. It is not just in sports that we rally around the strong man, the winner, but in politics and in business. The stronger personality usually wins. But Greenleaf proposed a different model in which serving led to trust and trust to leadership. This whole concept is in counter distinction to our usual understanding of leadership. The weight of responsibility may rest on the leader and the responsibility chain of command will show the leader at the top of the pyramid. However, when it comes to function, the leader is out front, leading by example and leading by doing. But, when the issue of power is shown graphically, the leader is at the bottom, empowering the organization, rather than ruling by taking power from the people in the structure.

Leadership Positions

Jack Dunigan of Leadership Ministries has shown leadership in three organizational forms.

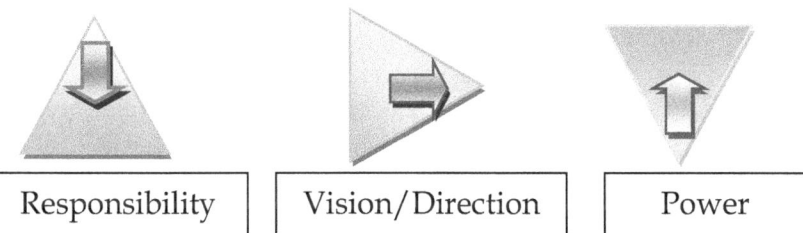

| Responsibility | Vision/Direction | Power |

In Responsibility, the leader is at the top, delegating responsibility downward through the organization. The objective is to place responsibility as close to the people as possible.

In Vision and Direction, the leader is out front, leading the troops, so to speak, and focusing the vision.

In terms of Power, the leader is at the bottom of the structure, empowering upward, constantly releasing power to points of responsibility so tasks can be accomplished.

The error of much of today's corporate leadership is that power is accumulated at the top and responsibility is given downward, creating a disparity between power and responsibility. Responsibility for the task cannot be accomplished until power matches the degree of responsibility given. On the other end, accumulated power at the top without responsibility is abusive and damages everyone in the chain of command.

Leadership and Greatness

Steven Covey popularized the concept of primary greatness and secondary greatness. In his writings on the subject he gives examples of those who are great because they are good and lead by serving. Mother Teresa is an example of servant leadership and of greatness that comes from a quality of service, competence of performance, and goodness given to others.

Conversely, we all know of famous people who are great, not because of any character quality they have expressed, but simply because they have accomplished a feat, risen to fame by some means, or have a talent. Characteristic of this category are the Hollywood famous, who have found notice from the public for their acting, singing, or outlandish behavior. The illusion of greatness is somehow assumed of the famous and we look to them for advice on matters of life, which of course many obviously know nothing about.

This same phenomenon exists in our political arena. We all know of the politician who is famous or powerful and, if we are not careful, we confer greatness upon them simply because of their fame. We are willing to dismiss their character flaws and lack of judgment in their personal lives, because they are 'great' and as such must be honored.

However, fame is but secondary greatness, and that is only because of some ability the person may have, not because they are in fact, good. Primary greatness is found in those who, regardless of fame, exhibit a model of life that can be followed with a certain exactness, because of the principles they have articulated, and the character they have as a person. These are harder to find because of their lack of fame, but are the ones we need to lead us.

Do not confuse power with greatness. Great people seldom seek power, while powerful people are seldom great. Yet we tend to elect the powerful and the egocentric to public office and then expect them to act in our best interest. They are powerful to begin with because they seek power and seek to rule rather than serve. If rewarded for their behavior, what do we expect them to do? What they will do is persist in their behavior and redouble their efforts.

Take a look at our founding fathers.

> George Washington was a General, scarred by the winds of war and the challenges of battle. He was by trade a surveyor and worked in the family agricultural business.

> Thomas Jefferson was a philosopher and business leader whose writings influenced the American and French revolutions.

Benjamin Franklin was a leading author, printer, political theorist, politician, postmaster, scientist, musician, inventor, satirist, civic activist, statesman, and diplomat.

At the time of the convention, 13 individuals were businessmen, merchants, boaters, or shippers: Blount, Broom, Clymer, Dayton, Fitzsimons, Gerry, Gilman, Gorham, Langdon, Robert Morris, Pierce, Sherman, and Wilson. Six were major land speculators: Blount, Dayton, Fitzsimons, Gorham, Robert Morris, and Wilson. Eleven speculated in securities on a large scale: Bedford, Blair, Clymer, Dayton, Fitzsimons, Franklin, King, Langdon, Robert Morris, Charles Cotesworth Pinckney, and Sherman. Twelve owned or managed slave-operated plantations or large farms: Bassett, Blair, Blount, Butler, Carroll, Jenifer, Mason, Charles Pinckney, Charles Cotesworth Pinckney, Rutledge, Spaight, and Washington. Broom and Few were small farmers.

Nine of the men received a substantial part of their income from public office: Baldwin, Blair, Brearly, Gilman, Jenifer, Livingston, Madison, and Rutledge. Three had retired from active economic endeavors: Franklin, McHenry, and Mifflin. Franklin and Williamson were scientists, in addition to their other activities. McClurg, McHenry, and Williamson were physicians, and Johnson was a university president. Baldwin had been a minister, and Williamson, Madison, Ellsworth, and possibly others had studied theology but had never been ordained.

This profile of occupations is in distinct contrast to our political leaders of today. The dominant occupation of today's politician is lawyer: 215 members (159 in the House and 58 in the Senate) have worked in some aspect of law during their career, whether as an attorney, paralegal, policy analyst, or bureaucratic official, with 180 members of the House and 58 of the Senate holding Juris Doctor degrees.

The contrast is, in the case of our founding fathers, who are noteworthy because they were people of the community that elected them. They were statesmen first and foremost, regardless of their occupation. They were serious students of philosophy and history and understood government from both the trust position they had earned and the bitter scars of conflict with tyrannical systems. They were renowned in their communities before they were ever elected to office. They were not career politicians without trade, craft or occupation.

They served without pay, for the most part, until they were elected and even when in office, served as a part time servant, relying on their continued occupation of trade for financial support. Being elected to office did not elevate their lifestyle or benefit them economically. They went into public service to serve, not to profit. Their financial success was from their occupations not from the power that came to them as a politician.

These were a different sort of people than those we elect today. They were men of accomplishments, or letters, and serious scholars. They were not pop culture icons of fame who articulate great promises but foundationally are devoid of character, principle, and goodness. Yes, we elect those who have achieved name recognition, but their greatness is secondary, not primary. If we are going to have leaders with qualities beyond what we tend to have, it is incumbent upon "we the people" to rethink our mindset and our willingness to settle for less than primary greatness. We have to take charge of our destiny by demanding that our leaders be philosophically sound, fiscally sane, and they must have exhibited the seed of greatness by their character and service.

Chapter Seven

Less is More

A search of the internet will show hundreds of ideas as to why nations fall. History shows the rise and fall of many nations and cultures, from Babylon, to the modern Soviet Union. While opinions vary, they all seem to include certain parallels. Below is a discussion of a few of them that have no doubt had a major influence on the stability of nations and serve as warning to us in our current existence as a nation.

1. Morals and Values

Charting the course of superpowers of the past we cannot ignore the issue that is raised by most historians. Most nations rise through the Herculean efforts of an industrious people, who are self sufficient and hard working. These people toil in the fields to provide for food, and work to build their habitation and the boundaries of their personal property, whether real estate or business based. The end result is they prosper and the community around them prospers with them. They have little or no leisure time and no vices to succor their strength and resolve. They are driven to survive and to prosper.

But as they do prosper, they leave to their children a better world, or so we tend to think, which provides for leisure time and entertainment opportunities. In time, this exploration of life outside of basic necessities leads to both legitimate entertainment and excesses that are destructive of both the individual and the community. As time goes on and the community learns to accommodate the value-free expressions and moral decline around it, the energy of the culture is given to that which does not produce but rather reduces the people involved. In this theory of cultural effect, morals and values support creativity and the production of goods and services, while leisure debauchery saps the strength of the culture and turns it into nonproductive pleasures that destroy rather than create.

It is not difficult to see this pattern in many fallen empires of the past.

2. Economics

All great super nations of the past started with the same economic status. They all had nothing to start with. Wealth is created not given. The progress of wealth starts with the industrious and energetic, working and building, and with a government that is small and attendant to the affairs of the people. As cottage industries become factories and factories become industries, wealth flows to the nation and the government that serves it.

But at some point, there is a natural shift in common with all fallen nations. At some point, the government of the nations becomes more than the end result of the industrious. It stops focusing on the support of the wealth builders and turns to try to solve the problems of those who consume rather than those who produce. As government programs grow to deal with the less fortunate who do not produce, that government has to find a way to support the redistribution of the wealth. In doing so it rewards the nonproductive with the efforts of the productive. While this seems to be a morally affirming policy, the end result is that those who consume increase in size and also increase the amount they consume, requiring more and more from those who produce.

While this is a simple equation on paper, it is less obvious in the actual function of a society. It is not hard to predict the end result, however. As the needs of the nonproductive exceed the supply of the producers, and as the government grows to accommodate programs of subsistence, the entire system crumbles. This directly relates to the motto of Al-Anon - Support success, don't support failure. This presumes the average person can be a producer and be successful and is best served by being responsible for their own life. But the end of the trail of supporting the nonproductive, is the paternalistic assumption that most people are too stupid and incapable of taking care of themselves and need a superior government program to take care of them.

The theory here is, when a nation and its government makes more promises of support than it can confiscate with a reasonable tax base, the entire structure falls.

3. Agriculture

Most historians list agriculture as one of the reasons nations fall. All great nations start from an agricultural base focused on the production and harvest of agricultural products. Not all areas of the world are as fertile as others and not all agricultural pursuits can grow all of the produce that may be desired, but as a foundational base for the economy of a nation, agriculture is always present. You simply must feed the people.

For many, however, the kind of labor that is required to produce from the earth is not desirable. It is hard work. To accomplish this task, many nations have resorted to the use of slaves or immigrant workers, which may amount to the same thing. To the degree that the numbers in this labor base is equal to the need, there is not a problem. But when the numbers of people needed for the task exceed the need, there is a problem of supporting those who are thus unemployed. There is also the conflict of cultures that exists when the numbers of those who come in to do the task, do not merge into the culture.

Some historians list this as a major influence on the fall of the Roman Empire and other super powers of the past. If the nation cannot maintain a central focus and culture, then the culture loses definition and focus and the community mindset is lost in a multi-cultural mess.

Yet, the maintenance of an agricultural base is essential to feed the people of any culture, large or small, grand or insignificant. If the agricultural needs are imported, then the producing nation has the power and some control of the importing nation. But if the work of agriculture is given to another culture within the nation, then the risk is the dilution of the central culture and the ultimate fall of the nation.

4. Loss of Freedom

When any society, culture, or nation reaches the saturation point of total control and the resulting loss of freedom, the end result is rebellion. The desire for freedom is genetically implanted in the human soul. When that desire is crushed and when the prospects for freedom become hopeless, productivity decreases and anger increases. The end result is either the refusal to produce or revolt.

Many of the great nations of history have ended by revolt of the masses who simply cannot endure the tyranny of control. Most of those nations try to pacify complaints of their people by promising reforms and change. When that fails, which it inevitably will, then the only means of control is force. History is replete with stories of the use of force to control the people with the objective of the power base remaining in control. These are the stories of raw power, taken beyond the legitimate scope of the responsibility to govern. Revolution is also inevitable when tyranny fails to provide for the needs of the people.

The process is simple. The more a government tries to do for the people, the more it needs from the people. The more it needs from the people, the more control it has to exert. The more control it exerts, the less productive the people become. It is a downward spiral of inefficiency that ends in the destruction of the culture.

5. Corruption in the Government

The corruption of power is not something that might happen; it is something that happens automatically when power exceeds responsibility. Human nature is such that we tend to confuse privileges of power with our identity. When we make and enforce the law, we tend to believe we are the law.

I have personally encountered this phenomenon in police work. When an officer can understand they represent the law, they can then depersonalize the negative responses of the element they deal with and dismiss those responses. That is, the speeder will, in many cases, become mad at the officer who stops them for their violation, rather than being angry at themselves for doing it. This misplaced sense of responsibility is common in the job of law enforcement. If the officer understands the process, then they cannot personalize the reactions and continue to do their job. But if officers position themselves as being the law, then the reaction is toward them personally and an angry response is the result.

At any level of leadership, the temptation is to believe that the role is the person; that is, to accept either the accolades or the criticism as something deserved or to be rejected. The greatest test in life is the test of success. To handle praise, success, position, wealth, or any means of power can become destructive. Politicians often forget that the power comes from the people and begin to see people as an element they need to control in order to maintain power. In whatever form or level this becomes the case, when the power begins to exceed the legitimate need for it to meet responsibility, corruption exists.

Governments easily shift from service as a motivation to regarding their power as deserved. Then, because they enjoy the perks of power, they yield to the motivation of power itself. The shift of mindset is simple and hardly even recognized. From a sincere desire to serve and make a difference, leaders can begin to see the frailty of humanity and to think of themselves as smarter than those they serve, better than those they serve, and worthy to lead because of their superiority. Certainly, working with and for people can feed cynicism thereby promoting a view of the human race as basically stupid and not able to govern themselves. But when that elitism becomes an identity, the leader is corrupt and their decisions are damning.

As unreasonable as our foundation for government seems to be, it affirms that the people, whether deserving or not, smart or not, capable or not, have the basic responsibility for self government. When government presumes to take that foundation away from the people, creating an intrusive system of controls to guarantee success for their constituency, destruction of the entire nation will be the result.

Other Reasons...

Various historians and writers have listed additional reasons why nations fall, and there are many contributing factors. I contend however, that the core reasons have to do with the position that responsibility and power hold in the culture. When the government removes responsibility from the individual and reduces the value of private property and private enterprise by taking, that power to the top, the culture has entered the bell curve of decline.

Chapter Eight

Security and Control

One of the most powerful charges in our founding documents is the challenge to resist the overreaching power of government. The Declaration of Independence not only permits the control of government but requires it:

> *But when a long train of abuses and usurpations, pursuing invariably the same Object evinces a design to reduce them under absolute Despotism, it is their right, it is their duty, to throw off such Government, and to provide new Guards for their future security.*

The premise is, left to its own nature; government will pursue power at the expense of freedom and ultimately enslave the constituency it is charged with serving. The tendency is for those elected to go to the Capitol and think that by creating more laws, they are accomplishing something. But with generation after generation of accumulated legislation, the Law of Progressive Density takes over and the vastness of legislation leaves no life to live without the oversight of fallible government. Freedom is lost in the maze of law.

In physics:

Density is defined as the ratio of an object's mass to its volume. You can express this mathematically as density (abbreviated with the Greek symbol rho) is equal to mass (m) divided by volume (V).

Density increases either with increasing mass or with decreasing volume. As density increases, speed and mobility are lost.

In social terms, the laws of physics have a parallel expression. As a society increases in length of time, it tends to increased density and reduced rates of progress and productivity. If the responsibility for this slow down is given away to government and government attempts to compensate by growing larger and doing more for the people, it will inevitably collapse into itself by the sheer weight of its mass and the lack of speed (effect). This is what I have called the Law of Progressive Density. It is the loss of mobility and productivity because of the accumulation of power, size and the loss of objectivity and flexibility.

The process is that the human family has a variety of needs and desires and some of them are conflicting. We want security and look to what we perceive as being over us, to provide it. The end result of this process is that we do not find security at all but bondage and control. It has been said that the course of human history is of human kind seeking security at the expense of slavery. We seem to need authority for reasons we do not understand. Possibly it is our fear and insecurity by which we presume others know better than we do or that the world we are placed into is far beyond our comprehension or mastery and so we give over our power to those who tell us that they can secure the world for us. In any event, history is filled with the stories of the king and the dictator who promise more than they can ever give and end up in control, without the wherewithal to actually meet the needs of the people.

It is with this in mind that our founding fathers cautioned us to limit the power and scope of government. Yes, there are people who are smarter than I, or than most of us, yet to give them the responsibility and the power to take care of me is counter to the natural order of things. The natural order is that we each take responsibility for our life and live it as best we see fit. The earth is not a stingy taskmaster but yields a harvest in multiple of what is sown. The law of harvest is that by working the earth we invest what is planted and receive multiple in return. Whatever the effort or enterprise, the principle is the same.

The premise is that all men are created equal in the degree of responsibility and in the power to fulfill it. That does not guarantee equal intelligence, equal rewards or equal outcome. Free enterprise garners its critics from the fact that the rewards of life are not guaranteed and the effect of the free market does not distribute an equal portion to all. But to move for central planning and an equal distribution of results always kills the human spirit, stifles the ingenuity of the individual and reduces us to a reliance on government to control the outcome of our effort. Government, when it enters the free market, can do one thing and one thing only - control the result and thus kill the motivation of the system.

My Dad had a very simple view of economic success. He would encourage us to never envy the success of others but to learn how they did it and then emulate them. He often said that the best thing you can do for the poor was to not become one of them. This general theme of personal responsibility drove him to be a model of how to overcome physical handicaps and cultural bigotry to make life work and to not offer excuses.

The trade off in life is that you can increase your security and reduce your fear by purchasing it with loss of control over your own life. The more you fear, the more control you tend to give away. The problem is, once you find out that those who promise to give you security are not doing so, it is difficult, if not impossible, to get it back. Power given away, tends to remain under the ownership of those to whom it was given. They don't easily give it back.

It's the old story of the chickens in the fence. You can put them in confinement and clip their wings, and as they try to fly away, they will crash into the fence and not escape. Then, after that conditioning process is complete, you can take down the fence and they will not try to fly anymore. They are under control.

We are not arguing for anarchy here. The confines of law are legitimate when erected where they are supposed to be. The old adage is, your freedom to swing your fist ends where my nose begins. There is a legitimate function in law and government. We do need the protection of the law, from those who, because of their lack of internal character, are destructive of others. There is a basic core of law that most all societies have adopted and is universal in nature. Violence against others, unless in self defense, is socially unacceptable in all cultures.

There are those who lack the ability to govern themselves, because of their lack of parameters and self control. It is the lawless for which laws are made. And, in the administration of these legitimate rules of behavior, those who enforce the law need the power to carry out their responsibilities. It is not law and constraint that is evil, it is the raw power taken beyond the legitimate responsibilities of enforcement that is the issue.

We blame the abusive for their illegitimate use of power, but there is another element we must pay attention to. It is the means by which that power is achieved. It is taken from those who are weak and fearful, but it is taken because we offer it up in our search for security.

I entered police work just before the Miranda decision forced law enforcement officers to advise suspects of their rights. When the decision came down, police officers from all over were complaining about the lawyers, the courts and the Supreme Court that issued the opinion. In several of those discussions, I was not well received when I postulated that the real culprit, the primary ones to blame in the chain of events leading to the decisions, was ourselves - the police, who allowed for the excesses that brought about the reaction and the decision.

So also where political corruption and excess power is accumulated, it is we who give the power to the abuser who need to bear our own blame. We have not limited the powerful in that we have given to them the excesses of power by our own need for benefits and services, rather than face our own responsibilities to take care of ourselves.

A study of cultures and nations of the past shows a variety of ways in which peoples have organized their social structures. We borrow much from the Greeks and the Romans, possibly because they left written records of their structures and way of life, but also because their structures in some form are the republics that we emulate. Those structures provided for a free economy, personal property and human rights to some degree. These concepts are not unheard of in human history, although they are the exception to the 'might makes right' structures of unrestrained power.

What we seem to fail to understand is that the socialist and communistic structures of history, although on the surface providing pluralistic leadership, are dictatorial none-the-less. Whenever the providence of government sacrifices individual liberties and individual property rights for the sake of the whole culture, it is doomed to failure by the sheer weight of its existence.

One of the remarkable lessons of history is that those social structures of history which pushed the decision making responsibility the furthest out in the structure, seemed to have greater peace and prosperity. Israel is one of the first recorded structures that developed a 'grass roots' system of authority. Aaron advised Moses that he could no longer judge all the people by himself, because he was sitting in judgment from early morning to late night and was worn out. So Moses appointed captains of 50's, captains of 100's and so forth and delegated to them the responsibility of adjudicating conflict in the camp.

> From A. D. 449, the date of the invasion, to 597, the landing of St. Augustine, the Saxon continued heathen, and transformed the political system of his Teutonic home, with its *civitas, pagus and vicus,* into the Saxon system of shire, hundred and township, which was the Saxon state in Teutonic mould. The epitome of the development of the Saxon organism from the seventh to the eleventh century is thus described by Dr. Stubbs:
>
>> "The people occupy settled seats; the land is appropriated to separate townships, and in these certain portions belong in entire possession to allodial owners, whilst others are the common property of the community; and there are large unappropriated estates at the disposal of the nation. Each of these townships has an organization of its own; for certain purposes the inhabitants are united by the mutual responsibility of the kindred; for others they are under the authority of their reeve, who settles their petty disputes, collects their contributions to the national revenue, leads the effective men to the fyrd, and with his four companions represents the township in the court of the hundred or in the folkmoot. The townships are not always independent; sometimes they are the property of a lord, who is a noble follower. He comes with the power of the king, with jurisdiction over the men of the township, and many of the rights which we associate with feudalism. Where, however, this is the case, the organization is of the same sort; the reeve is the lord's nominee, the moot is the lord's court, the status of the inhabitants is scarcely less than free, and their duties to the state are as imperative as if they were free.
>
> [1] [Tucker note #1] Taine's English Literature, 51.
> John Randolph Tucker, LL.D.
> Chicago, Callaghan & Co, 1899 (published posthumously)

Throughout human history, there have been challenges to authoritarian government and the exploration of both the rights of the people and the limits of governmental power. Yet, never has there been such a sweeping compilation of the principles of human rights, personal freedom and the control of government until the American Revolution and the Constitution of the United States. This noble experiment in building a nation is somewhat unique to human history and stands as an example of what mankind can be and what we can accomplish.

While some look at human history and ascribe the success of nations as the result of chance, of location, or of personalities, our founding fathers ventured to ascribe the prospects of success to the foundational principles and concepts that they laid in place in our beginnings. If this perspective has any basis in fact, then the success of the United States of America is not because of our ethnic origin, our location, or our being better or smarter than other peoples of the past, but on those foundations upon which we stand. If this is true, then the challenges to our foundations and our documents as being living documents, that is, subject to change, is indeed the enemy of our future.

Chapter Nine

The Shifting World View

With the shift of world view represented in our founding documents as to how power flows from bottom to top rather than top to bottom, there are other significant ramifications. They represent a sweeping change to our human view of reality. The problem is, we tend to lose the view over time. We are good at reverting to the views of societies past, if the new paradigm is not documented, articulated and passed down to newer generations.

I experienced one of the examples of this phenomenon in college. It was in the late 50's that communism was seen as a threat and Senator Joe McCarthy rose to prominence fighting what he saw as a Communist conspiracy to rule the world. Being young and inquisitive, I decided I should investigate for myself. So I found a copy of The Communist Manifesto in a local library and read it. At first I was taken by the sense of passion for the poor and the development of a social system by which equality was possible. Then, something struck me. At first I was critical of some conclusions Marx made, but then, I found myself questioning the entire premise. Before I was through, I was convinced that this was not just a benign alternative view of politics and economics; it was, in fact, a dangerous view of our world that was incompatible with our founding documents and with the Biblical view of reality.

First of all, it espoused a top down theory of power. That is in contrast to our foundations. Secondly, it espoused a limited system of value as the bottom line of economics. This I could not buy and the reasons are as follows:

A New View of Our Earth

One of the predominant themes of economics prior to our revolution and the sweeping changes into our world during that time was that of a limited pie. If you took two pieces, then someone was left with none. If you prospered, then others would be left without their needs being met. Economics in this world view is that of the zero/sum base line. That is, the pie is limited in size and application. If someone gets more than others, it is because they have taken more than their fair share. This is the basic philosophy, heard loudly today as power brokers call for everyone to pay their fair share. It focuses on those who have more, and assumes that since they have more, they are obligated to pay for more of our social services.

But our founding documents propose that we all have the right to pursue success. It has, as a base line, an assumption that everyone can succeed without anyone being the victim of that success. The world view here is that productivity adds to the base line, rather than extracts from it. The paradigm shifts from a fixed volume of value to an infinite source of value, waiting to be created by the ingenuity and creativity of the participants.

The best argument for the non-zero/sum view of economics and value in our world is the sheer mass of the increase of population on the planet. If the value pie is limited and determinate, then we would have all starved to death ages ago. Therefore we conclude that the problem with limited economics is with the imagination and creativity of the human family, not with a limited supply of resources from the earth.

Socialism and communism are based on the zero/sum philosophy of value. Their view of success is to envy it and suspect it of being unfair. It never occurs to someone, trapped in that thought process, to imagine they can emulate the successful rather than envy them.

That all men are created equal in value is the premise. That all will be successful is the hope. However, nothing is guaranteed economically because, the government is not given the power of central planning and distribution. An accompanying premise is that private property is assured. The means of success is assumed to be private enterprise, productivity, and creativity. These are the building blocks laid on top of the freedom we are given. Anyone can have it, but they have to go get it. It is not given to them by governmental or constitutional edict. The government cannot guarantee success because it does not have the power to do so. It is limited to the powers specifically given in the Constitution. All other power is reserved for the private sector and individual creativity.

Success cannot be guaranteed by government, nor distributed by government. When government starts to deal in this arena, it always messes it up. The premise is that the natural created order of things drives people to success by their own initiative. When government enters the scene, it converts that sense of ownership of success from a personal prerogative to a government right. This is the socialist view of economics and human rights and strips the individual of the motivation to create and succeed.

A New View of Social Structure

There was another powerful element at work in the founding of this nation. It is how society in general is viewed. Under the king or dictator, people are seen as property, much like real estate or agricultural products or any other 'thing' in the social or economic structures. If all is owned by the ruler it is therefore the ruler's responsibility to take care of them.

Today's resurgence of this perspective of humanity comes to us from the fields of sociology and psychology as scientists study the effect of certain environments on people groups. I often wonder if those who study the effects of environment on a subculture of people ever consider that the subculture within the environment may have created the environment they are in rather than the reverse? But then, what do I know?

With the founding of this nation, and within the convergence of several paradigm shifts, there emerged a new way of looking at the nation. The basic premise was the worth of the individual and the value added when the individual takes responsibility for progress, success and care of one's self. While nomadic tribes survived in the hunter/gather culture as a group, basically a nuclear family of extended generations, the industrial revolution threw us into cities and subcultures within cities. It is here the government thought it had to consider what to do with those who were behind the curve economically and socially.

The problem with this shift of attention is that the basis of our system of freedom, economically, spiritually, religiously, and in all ways, is that we are free to make determinations for our lives and to reap the rewards personally. If freedom equates to gain and success then poverty is not primarily a social issue, but the result of how freedom is handled by the individual. This is in stark contrast to the socialistic view of people that assigns social causes to economics, productivity, etc. The end result is, we have become a nation with mixed philosophies of focus and an ambivalent approach to life together. You cannot have it both ways and expect progress to occur. If freedom results in progress then freedom of the individual has to be the bottom line in the governmental approach to its administration. We have to have space, legally and environmentally to explore the determinations that are made within the individual.

The question is, where are the determinations made? Does the power to decide one's goals, dreams, and activities rest with the individual or with the government? Ah, but the argument is obvious: What if the decisions of the individual are ignorant and lead to failure? The answer is painfully simple. Some will, and the same equality of freedom that gives us each the right and the responsibility for self determination, will end up with an unequal result. That is the down side of freedom. But to opt to eliminate the risk of failure and the tragedy of errant decisions is to empower government to be the caretaker of us all and to throw away the freedom that has made us great. Again, you cannot have it both ways.

The Assumption of Elitism

There is another convergent paradigm shift in the founding of this nation. It is the rejection of the right of the elite to govern over the ignorant. The American Revolution was a rejection of the premise of an intelligentsia who had the responsibility, right, and ability to rule the people and run their lives.

- "I predict future happiness for Americans if they can prevent the government from wasting the labors of the people under the pretense of taking care of them." -- Thomas Jefferson
- "My reading of history convinces me that most bad government results from too much government." -- Thomas Jefferson

The whole concept of limited government is to provide for the defense of the nation and to seek to govern in truth and liberty, a people who had the space to create their own lives and roles in society. The limits of government are exceeded when any politician thinks they know better how to make decisions for the individual than the individual does.

Tyranny first happens in the mind of the leader who believes they know what is best for the masses, and then gravitates to legislation to govern the behavior of those who seek the freedom to create their own life. It is this perspective, of limited government and the presumption of personal responsibility that is the foundation of our nation.

Of course this is not an argument for anarchy. The rule of law is always a context to protect everyone from the violence of those who would be predators on society. It is, however, an argument for a reasoned and limited approach to government free from the hubris of elitists who presume they can and should tell everyone else what to do and where to go. The issue here is control versus freedom. The more control, the less freedom. The more legislation, the less we enjoy personal determination. This continuum of cause and effect is inextricably linked together.

The continuum also has economic ramifications. Economic freedom produces a free enterprise system of success, but top down control of that system erodes its success and limits its creativity. The more government influences the free market, the less it becomes a free market. The more government tries to take care of people, the less people take care of themselves. This is the principle of social dynamics on which our nation was founded. The perception is that by limiting government and making the individual responsible, success would be the result. It is hard to argue with this premise when looking back at the success of the nation, yet, it is hard to understand why we have drifted so far from our acceptance of this basic fact.

Maurice R. Stein sees society evolving to better meet human needs when he says, "Humanist sociology views society as a historically evolving enterprise that can only be understood through the struggle to liberate human potentialities." When that enterprise, the betterment of society, is given to the government, the end is not a better society but a bigger government and the overreaching of the limits of the powers of government our forefathers presumed to stop. When that betterment is the provision of an open ended opportunity to all the individuals within the society, then freedom produces.

Secular humanists believe social activism will bring about a culture of universal self-actualization. Curtis Williford Reese of the American Humanist Association says, "Informed and active people can make of society what they want it to become." Secular Humanist disdain for modern society reflects an open distrust of all traditions and a desire to abandon or rework all existing social institutions. For the elitist, the corporation and the successful are enemies of those who are excluded from getting their piece of the pie. They never consider that the excluded individuals have the right and the ability to make more pies.

Chapter Ten

A ~~New~~ Old Social Construct

Formal vs. Informal

The basic social construct of humanity, since the beginning of time, has been the family. The nuclear family is the foundation stone of all other relationships, both formal and informal. As goes the family, so goes the culture.

Join me for a few minutes, on a journey into the past. I want to expose you to my world. I want to take you back to my criminal justice class at Truckee Meadows Community College in Reno, Nevada. The class room is usually full because it has become a popular class. We have fun discussing things and setting up possibilities. We use the text book, but it hardly defines the class. You see, I am basically an informal person. Let me illustrate.

The text has led us to the section on juvenile justice and we are told, because of problems of the past, federal law prohibits juveniles from being housed in adult jail facilities. Juveniles are to be provided with a separate system of justice and separate housing facilities under the presumption that it is dangerous for them to be thrown into a jail cell with Bubba the rapist or the influence of adult criminals. It is not the place for kids.

The problem this creates is that not all communities are equipped with these separate facilities nor do they have the budget to build them. Then I turn the class's attention to a rural community just over 100 miles from our town named Lovelock. Lovelock is a rural agricultural community of about 2,000 people, a couple of churches, a motel or two and several bars. It is a delightful place of families, wherein community activities in a context of deep relationships and familiar history reside.

In the classroom we set up a scenario. Johnny, a teenager of about 15 years of age, is out with some friends one night, infused with testosterone, feeling mischievous and looking for something to do. They decide, mostly on Johnny's urging to go for a joy ride out by the river, where they usually hang out and fish in the daylight hours. But, of course, they do not have a driver's license and they do not have a car. This is of little consequence since in this rural trusting community, someone will have left their keys in their car. So they prowl around a bit and finally find the car with the keys in it, next door to Johnny's house.

They push the car 100 feet or so down the street, so the noise of its starting does not wake the neighbors and off they go, carefree and mobile. The problem is, down by the river sits Officer Elroy, patrolling for (you guessed it), juveniles who should be home in bed. Now we have a problem. The letter of the law says that juveniles cannot be housed in adult facilities, but this is seldom a problem because, the city jail has two signs. One reads, "City Jail," while the other reads, "Juvenile Hall." Problem solved. When an adult is jailed, one sign is hung up and when a juvenile is incarcerated the other sign is hung up.

But on this occasion, there is already a drunk driver in the city jail cell, so now we have a problem. Officer Elroy can set about building a new juvenile facility or he can, as the city has decided, use their contract relationship with Washoe County, in the City of Reno and take the errant kids there. However, Reno is over 100 miles away and Officer Elroy is the only officer on duty. He can call out another officer and create overtime for the city, which he has been instructed to not do except in emergencies, or he can leave the city and take them to Reno. This would involve driving two hours each way plus an hour for booking and coffee, leaving the city unprotected for five or more hours. This is the formal and legal means of handling the situation.

My guess is that Officer Elroy is going to resort to an informal solution. He will call the parents of the kids and, after completing his paperwork, release them to their parents. My question to the class is then: Which solution is better and more effective? There is always one person in the class who will affirm that, regardless of the inconvenience, you have to follow procedures and follow the law. The rest of the class will affirm that, the end result is the same - the teens are going to have to face the judge anyway, regardless of how they get there.

The point I make in all this is, that in the city we would handle this differently. The teens would go to juvenile hall, be housed with other offenders, and then be released to parents. They would face a formal juvenile court process, be sentenced and their offense recorded in the juvenile system. Their association would be with other offenders and their process would be formal. The psychological implications would be quite different than the informal process of the rural community. In the rural setting the teens would face their parents first of all, and then would have to face the neighbor. Next they would go before the juvenile hearing officer who might, in this rural setting and tight knit community deal with the sentencing quite differently than in the city. The difference is formal authority or informal authority.

The class, at this point is buzzing with ideas of what all this means and most of them are saying, "If it is me, give me the formal system. I would never want to face my dad with this." The difference in context is, most rural communities are comprised of nuclear families with mom, dad, a dog, a cat, and several siblings. The primary authority in the teen's life is the family. But in the city, the family is dead. There may be no dad. Mom is worn out trying to work and take care of the affairs of the broken family is left to her. The resources of authority, absent the traditional family, are formal, legal and impersonal.

The existence of our juvenile justice system in this nation is only some 60 plus years old. In prior generations, the state was not set up to deal with juvenile justice. Justice for children was administered by the family and within the family. The concept of parens patria, or the state as the parent is relatively new to our culture. The concept has been around in the law forever, but the administration required no separate system, staff or facilities because of the strength of the informal family system. I would also argue that this informal relational system of justice was more effective and less damaging because it was underpinned by love and genuine concern for the child's life and future.

There are other examples of the informal administration of authority as opposed to the systems of formal justice. The Andy Griffith Show is one of my favorite examples of informal authority. Mythical though it may be, it is not far off from what exists in some communities. One of my favorite episodes is of the businessman whose car breaks down in Mayberry and Gomer has to order parts from the city to be able to fix it. This means that the businessman will miss his important appointment and he simply cannot do that. So, in a fit of conflicting urges, he steals Gomer's truck to get to his appointment. Alas, he is caught before he gets out of town and Barney is ready to take his one bullet from his shirt pocket and usher the desperado into jail. He has finally found a need for his propensity for formal authority.

Andy has another idea and decides to take the fellow home with him where Aunt Bee feeds him some good home cooking and then the family settles down to an evening of guitar playing, singing, and finally they put the fellow up in their guest room. The next day the car is fixed, the fellow is free to go about his business, but something has happened. The loving relationships of this community have eroded his need to rush into the city and hurry about to take care of business. His reality has been transformed by an informal encounter with the goodness of Mayberry.

Yes, I know it is only a movie script, but it illustrates a real life principle. To the degree that we can administer informal authority, we will avoid formal authority. One of the best real life examples of this principle happened a few miles from our house. An Indian Tribe a few miles out of town had a reputation of going through Chiefs of Police regularly. The last one they had hired came in to clean up the tribe. He was a no nonsense, law and order advocate who laid down the law. He stopped traffic violators by seeing that tickets were issued for everything including parking awkwardly on the rural streets. He arrested people, regardless of relationships within the tribe and in short order had created chaos which resulted in a reaction he did not see coming. Within a few months the Tribal council convened and he was fired. Why? For doing what he thought was his job - administering formal authority.

A friend on the Reno Police Department thought about applying for the job. It would be a pivotal move in his career ...if he succeeded. He would have a Chief of Police line on his resume and he could then move to other openings in the state that paid better. But the prospects of success were not bright. So he called and we met and talked. I shared with him my perspective of the situation and of human cultures in general. Our authority systems are much like an iceberg. Only a third is visible, while the rest, the greater mass, is beneath the waterline.

That portion which is visible represents our codified laws and regulations - formal authority. This tribe had federal law, state law and tribal law all codified and the books were in the police department and the judge's chambers. These were the visible representation of formal authority. But, more so than in most cultures, the real power was not in the formal systems but in the unwritten traditions and tribal relationships. To ignore that fact and resort to the formal administration of law was not going to work. It might be legally right, but it was a relational offense and a dishonoring of the real point of authority. The two thirds of the iceberg that is unseen but far more powerful was the informal relationships of the culture.

My friend then asked, "How then, can anyone outside of that culture succeed in administering the law?" I proposed that the first order of business was not to establish the formal position of having the power to administer the law, but to earn the right to be part of the community. I ventured that if I would take that position, I would order my police officers to put a basketball in the trunk of their car as a part of their standard equipment. Then I would tell them to go out in the streets of the community and when they saw a group of teens gathered in a park or school grounds, rather than policing them, I would tell them to park their car, take off their duty belt with gun, cuffs and other instruments of violence and take out the ball and go challenge the kids to a game.

We talked about the Mayberry model of police work for this rural setting and discussed other ways of discovering the informal expectations and of standing with the community rather than trying to stand over the community. This would be an adaptation of community oriented policing in which neither he nor I had any previous experience.

He took the job. He discovered ways to stand with the community and to solve problems, most often without the use of formal authority. The crime rate of the community plummeted, and he remained at the post far longer than any chief of police they had ever had. When he finally left his position, the community threw a party for him and mourned his leaving. To this day, he remains a consultant to the tribe and to other tribes and communities on how to do law enforcement in the small community.

I propose that government in our nation started out on a relational basis. The communities dealt with problems as they arose, using their best judgment and common sense. They created laws based on the common law that they were familiar with. That is, that which is commonly understood as inappropriate is the rule of law. This assumes that all people, in most cultures, have a common expectation of what is right and wrong. The codification and formal documents of law follow the presumption that right and wrong do exist and that the average person will know and understand these principles without having to codify them. But, to eliminate any misunderstanding, we decided to write them down, agree to them and follow them as the rule of law. The problem with written law is, it cannot cover every action or every circumstance. The secondary problem with law is, once written there are always unintended consequences. Those consequences happen when the law is administered by its letter without regard to its intent, or the spirit of the law. The problem is, when there are those who administer the law who are officious and use the power of their office beyond the responsibility intended. They become abusive, creating problems by administering the law which was created to solve problems, where no problem existed.

In a broader perspective, this becomes a larger problem the higher the level of authority. We have become a nation of programs, rules, regulations, and formal authority that has smothered informal relational authority. We cannot take independent action because we have become oriented to let the government take care of it. The poor do not relate to the family, the church, or a community's relational base. They rely on the government. The government is not only expected to take care of armies and highways but also Aunt Ethel who is elderly and needs care and old George, the town drunk. We have abandoned our duty to stick with the family and take care of our personal responsibilities and have given over that power to huge governmental bureaucracies that cost us a fortune to fund and whose effectiveness is far less than the informal community systems of relational authority administered in love.

Chapter Eleven

American Fundamentals

Who's On First?

"Sir, my concern is not whether God is on our side; my greatest concern is to be on God's side, for God is always right" **Abraham Lincoln**

It is no secret that the vast majority of our founding fathers were religious men. Looking through the quotes from any number of them will bring confirmation that they had a firm belief in God and a trust that the Creator of the universe was still in charge of the universe and of them.

Whether or not a person believes in God or has a religious foundation does not change the assumptions of our founding father, nor the philosophical stream from which our nation was founded.

Rush Limbaugh, the popular conservative talk show host has taken a lot of heat because of his saying, "with talent on loan from God." Those who react negatively see this as a statement of arrogance, while others laugh at the shock value Limbaugh seems fond of using, in the backhanded sarcasm of humor. The fact is, that is exactly how the people in the new world viewed themselves in relationship to God. For them, God was the only point of absolute authority and total power. Everyone else held the power of their responsibilities and the authority they were called to as an outgrowth of the delegation of power from God. They held a firm sense of submission to the will and authority of God. They understood that their talent, responsibility and power, was on loan from God.

Without that sense of submission to absolute authority, the human family tends to seek aggrandizement and become drunk with the presence of power. Where there are no limits to the accumulation of power, there is indeed arrogance and a sense of superiority over the people, who are simply too stupid or ignorant to take care of themselves. There is something good in any leader who has the humility to recognize they have position and power, intellect and knowledge, personality and talent, on loan from God. He who gave it will ask for an accounting and it is within this submissive context that leadership can function in a context of service, rather than in an assumption of the right to rule.

The question is, who's on first? That is, in the hierarchy of power, who holds the strings? Too often our leaders believe they have power because of who they are or what they know or because of their worth. In that sense, power is achieved. But if it is on loan from God it is only borrowed and has to be given back to the point from which it came. Authority is given to protect and to serve. It is a gift, not a right.

Authority is representative. The police officer is not the law, they represent the law. The judge is not the law, they only administer the law. Even the legislature is not the law; they are simply the point of response to a need for the protection of the law. No one in the chain of the authority of the law should ever be confused with the law itself, for they cannot be everywhere present, all knowing or all powerful. They are only representative of the nature of creation, expressed in codified documents.

Authority is also limited. All authority, regardless of how high it is in the structures of an organization or government, is limited. To the degree the one having the authority perceives that authority as unlimited they are abusive and out of order. The assumption of our founding fathers was, that the ultimate power of the Creator gave to all men certain rights and that no authority has the right or the ability to remove those rights. Properly limited authority will never move into a position of even addressing those rights. They are sacred to the individual in relationship to the Creator who gave them.

In this whole structure of power, responsibility and authority, the Founders accepted that there is a point of absolute authority and power, and that is the Creator God. Everyone else uses their abilities on loan from God and will ultimately give an accounting for how they handled those under their influence. When it is a question of who is first, it is not good to step forward to take God's place. Not good at all.

Chapter Twelve

What Constitutes Power?

Political power grows out of the barrel of a gun.

Political work is the life-blood of all economic work.

Politics is war without bloodshed, while war is politics with bloodshed.

Mao Tse Tung

In contrast to the general sentiment of our founding fathers, Mao believed that raw power, without the consent of the people, was the means of leadership. His life and conquests and the resulting famines in China are testimony to the efficiency of his theories. He believed that power was a top down matter and that the power of central planning and the political control of the economy were right.

This is the fallacy of the entire body of socialist thought. It assumes that if things are formally organized and controlled, progress can be made and that equality of outcome will be the result. But history provides another argument in contrast to these well meaning philosophies. To come to the conclusion that the welfare of the masses is in contrast to the welfare of the individual, and for the individual to succeed is is therefore bad for the masses does not work out well in practice.

To keep the individual from taking more than their share assumes a zero sum game, and limits the motivation of the individual to be upwardly mobile. To elevate the poor by bringing down the rich never works. The goal of economics is to provide opportunities for individual success that will allow all men to rise to the highest level of their competence. Thus the power of economics must always reside with the individual in the private sector and never with the government as the master of distribution. When the power of government determines individual success, then success will cease to exist.

> I know of no safe depository of the ultimate powers of the society but the people themselves; and if we think them not enlightened enough to exercise their control with a wholesome discretion, the remedy is not to take it from them but to inform their discretion.

Thomas Jefferson

To place the economy in the hands of government is to make a blanket rejection of the power of the people both to exercise sound judgment and to determine a reasoned course to their future. Yet, this policy of a private sector economy leaves risk intact and does not guarantee success. To guarantee equality of economic results does not evenly distribute wealth, but unevenly distributes poverty. Economics has to have the base of a willing seller and a willing buyer. To make blanket social determinations by government fiat destroys the uneven energy, creativity and drive of individuals. Self-determination is the backbone of any economic enterprise and, if we are wise, government shall be supportive of it rather than intrusive into it.

The power of government economic policy must remain ever focused on supporting the power of a free market and never the regulator of the enterprise of free men and their ingenuity.

> I have no fear that the result of our experiment will be that men may be trusted to govern themselves without a master.

> I predict future happiness for Americans if they can prevent the government from wasting the labors of the people under the pretense of taking care of them.

> Every government degenerates when trusted to the rulers of the people alone. The people themselves are its only safe depositories.

> Thomas Jefferson

Mao Tse Tung was right in a historic sense. That is, power has most often been exerted by the use of violence in forcing people to submit to the rule of the strongest person. But we have entered into a new social experiment in which that formula for success has been inverted and the assumption of the rule of force has been replaced by the assumption of the rule of the people, who hold the power. We stand in the middle of the American dream, in which freedom is not the absence of the law, but is the result of a law that has been determined by the people, not the king. The success of this inverted power structure has served well to show that Mao was wrong.

Power, in the relationship to the government of a nation, should never be by force but by the voluntary compliance with the law of the people for the people. The continued success of this noble experiment into self-governance shall be determined by our ability to enforce the law evenhandedly and fairly without increasing the burden of the law until it crushes the life from reasonable people.

They, who demonstrate against the rich, show a disregard for themselves as beggars at the doorstep of the very rich they resent. You cannot create success by bringing down the successful, but by stimulating every able bodied person to exert their personal power to step into the marketplace of economics and to bring something to the table of commerce worth the price they ask for it. Social success is determined by the individual participation in the economic game and the rise of everyone involved, not by the reduction of wealth from those who have it. To do otherwise will repeat the failure of every socialistic enterprise in history.

Chapter Thirteen

The Power of Money

The golden rule of economics is said to be: He who has the gold makes the rules. To some extent, this is exactly the case. Money represents power. Those who have it are able to hire and fire, set policy for their economic interactions, and to influence people and policy. Influence is power and those who have money are often in a position to influence the thinking and actions of the powerful.

The common misquote of the Biblical proverb is, "Money is evil!" But the scriptural reference says, "The love of money is a root of all kinds of evil." (Literal translation) Money, in and of itself is nothing. It is simply a piece of paper and ink that is used to exchange for goods and services. It is representative. It represents profit in the marketplace. It represents the value of the goods and services exchanged. It represents the skill with which its holder has negotiated their sphere of influence and their marketplace. And yes, it represents power.

Again, back to our premise, power is not evil any more than money, in and of itself, is evil. What is evil is the extending of power beyond legitimate responsibility. The evil is in the control over others beyond the legitimate and agreed upon price in the marketplace. There is nothing evil in the negotiations between the willing buyer and the willing seller. What may be evil in a given exchange is the marketing of weakness at the price of power. That is, when the weak are prey to the strong, death is the end result. But, there are two evil sides to the predator/prey analogy. One is the overpowering control that is brought to the table by the power broker. The other is the willingness by the weak to give over more power to them for the pittance that is accepted for the power exchanged.

Control does not come from the strong to the strong. Power might be exchanged between the strong and the strong, but the rewards of this kind of exchange are always from an equal position of strength. Control comes when the weak are willing to give over control and to become dependent on the strong. The evil inherent in this exchange is in both those who are willing to allow dependence and on those who solicit it.

In a political sense, we love to blame the evil politicians for the ever increasing control and regulations of government, but the equal opposite of that is that we the people have allowed our government to become too large and intrusive and it will remain so until we stop the train and get off. We are ultimately responsible for our own loss of power and the control of our own lives. This is also true in the world of economics. We have lost the understanding of 'caveat emptor,' - let the buyer beware. Blaming the evil corporation for taking advantage of people supports the evil of weakness in giving over power to them by those in the marketplace. If what they are doing is evil, then do not buy their products or use their services. Without customers, there is no power and no control.

One of our great problems is that in our distrust of the marketplace and our unwillingness to take responsibility for being a wary buyer, we give more power to the government to regulate and increase the price we pay as well as creating dependence, giving increased portions of our freedom and the free market into the hands of regulators. That is just how it works.

We are not saying that there should be no regulations and no moral context to the marketplace. What we are saying is that the more responsibility we give away in the arena of caveat emptor, the more control we invite. Power is not extracted without a price.

The Power of Money

The fact that money has power or represents power is a fact with which few would argue. Behind most politicians is the power of money. Elections are seldom equal in their financing. Those who have the money behind them are usually those who win. Usually, but not always. Once again, the problem is, seldom is there an exchange of power that is equal and without expectations and rewards. People with the power of money rarely give it away without some expectation of an advantage. The marketplace of value is not limited to the purchase of a product. Often what is purchased is influence and control. It might be said that when money is given there is always a hook inside. The money is only the bait to gain some point of control. If you take the money you also accept the expectation and the control it implies.

So the task, in the arena of money and politics, is to determine whether the expectations of the giver are consistent with the course of the taker and their ethical pursuits. If it is, and it further supports the path of the candidate, then there is certainly not an evil outcome. Both are mutually supportive of each other and the agreed upon course of action does not create dependency. Both win in the exchange. But when the politician is dangled like a marionette on the strings of the puppeteer, and is influenced to do what they are not pleased to do, then illegitimate control is present. The entire system of the free market of ideas and leadership is damaged.

The power of money can also be evil in how the employer treats, rewards and values their employees. The corporate sweat shop of the early industrial revolution or of the third world emerging economy is always repulsive to the sensitivities of any ethical and moral person. But the inverse of that scenario is also evil. When the unionization of the corporation shifts the power from the management to the power brokers of the union, there can also be an imbalance of the power and the control that damages the marketplace of the exchange of labor for an appropriate wage.

Companies are not started without the expectation of a profit. Profit is not evil. But to devalue the labor that contributes to the profit is unwise and can be evil. The ultimate balance of power within the labor/management continuum is that management values their employees and shares with them the fruit of their labor. The power to see that this is the case is within the hands of both management and labor. The company has no obligation to keep the person who does not contribute to the profit motive of the company. Likewise, the employee has no obligation to work for the company who devalues their contribution by the working conditions or the rate of pay. The leveling device for this equality of exchange can be the negotiations of an organized work force, or the pressure of the disruption of an unstable work force who simply will not work under the conditions given.

A new and growing phenomenon is seen in the American work force today. Some have labeled it the entitlement generation. It is seen in the employee who is first and foremost concerned with their benefits, how long they can have for a break and lunch and how easy the work will be. This entitlement mentality is a primary reason for attracting the immigrant population, who, coming from extreme poverty, are willing to work harder and longer than their spoiled counterpart. Yet, this also creates the problem of the company who is willing to barter away their responsibility to the labor force to take advantage of the worker who is willing to work for less pay and fewer benefits than the reasonable and expected wage. However you cut it, the ethical stand of both employee and employer has to be negotiated in such a way as to affirm the value of the company and the employee.

Finding a way to do that evenhandedly without an imbalance of power is the problem. It is here that the union has value, yet all too often, those who rise to the top in union power, become as unethical as those with whom they negotiate. Negotiations of power are always difficult and give rise to the evils of control, whether by those who lead without a service motivation or by the growth of government to control the private sector. How then shall these negotiations of power be handled? Is there a place for governmental oversight and the rule of law? Certainly there is in the creating of a context for equality of power. Yet the more intrusive the regulations the more it costs the company, the employee and the general marketplace of the product or service offered under the banner of the company.

To some degree, there will always be imbalance and imperfections in the system. Like all issues of responsibility, power and authority - it is best left to the lowest level of the relationships that are actually doing the working and the managing.

The ultimate answer may be in the words of my father who said:

- The best thing you can do for the poor is to not be one of them.
- Do not resent the rich. If you do, you will never be one of them. Rather learn from them.
- You can sell your labor, your goods or your services, but never give away your power.
- Never seek raw power. Rather seek responsibility and the power will come to you to do the task.
- Seek to influence rather than to take advantage of any man.

- To serve brings greater power than to control. Seek to serve, and the world will follow you.

Chapter Fourteen

The Power of Information

It was Alvin and Heidi Toffler who gave to us the concept of 'power shift.' In the early formations of power within human relationships, power was exerted by the strongest bully. Today, the bully is looked down on and despised. The caveman finally grew up and yielded his power to the shifting power base of agriculture. The asset value in being the bully leader was in personal strength. The power of the barrel of the gun was lost to some degree as power shifted in the agricultural age. Oh, they still exist, those bullies, but they have had to take a bath and put on a suit and tie. Whether or not one is a bully, may, to some degree, be in the eye of the beholder.

Where, for the caveman, assets were measured in terms of personal strength, in the agricultural revolution, assets were measured by one's ability to produce from the land and to raise the animals that were available. Power in the agricultural age, came through the ability to find the right soil, prepare it, water it and produce edible crops. The asset value was in the land and the attending to the land. A great influence in the power of agriculture was in the fertility of the land and the presence of water.

The industrial revolution shifted the power base again to those who could specialize and organize production and create an organized process in combination with an organized work force. This shifted the asset value to the ownership of fixed assets: Land, buildings, commodities, and other hard assets.

Over the past four or five decades we have seen another power shift in which the control and dissemination of information has become the new asset and the new power base. The proliferation of the personal computer and the availability of information have released information to the masses as never before. Huge companies that did not exist a generation ago, have risen to power simply by their ability to organize information and to market it as usable for companies and individuals. Even the power of the gun is in an army's ability to fight smart as opposed to the exertion of brute force. The power of technology and the power of the technological revolution are without dispute.

We are, however, moving into a crisis time in which those who are technologically savvy have accumulated power, while those who are not in tune with the technology of today are left behind. We live in a day where it is difficult, if not impossible to find any kind of job without some basic computer skills. While power is moving toward those who are on the cutting edge of this technological revolution, there are vast parts of our world which are left behind. The state of being left behind has consequences, both real and imagined. Those left behind in technical knowledge are also left behind in the shift of values and assets that follow the power curve. We are fast moving toward a conflict between those who have the power of technology and those who do not. That powerlessness and the resulting blame for the dichotomy is rising and will inevitably spill over into our relationship and our politics.

One of the problems, as money follows power, which it inevitably does, is the separation of our national subcultures into worlds that simply do not have the ability to communicate. Simultaneously with that separation is the social task of dealing with the accumulation of wealth on the one side and the loss of assets on the other. Politically we are already in the throes of conflict as to whether it is moral and right for money to flow toward power. While those who are the 'have nots' move into the resentment of their state, conflict is inevitable. The problem is, there is no solution for them, simply because the law of economics is that money moves toward power and that will never change.

We also find ourselves in the controversy as to what role government should play in the distribution of wealth and how moral it is for wealth to accumulate at certain points of advantage. When the government takes responsibility for the inequality of wealth it will ultimately fail, for it cannot stop the reasons for that accumulation or the lack of it. What it can do is focus on motivating those without the technological skills to gain them and develop them, for without these skills, they are doomed to be outside the stream of wealth that will inevitably flow toward those who have the knowledge and the power. Those who take the risks to create and to invent will always attract the flow of wealth. Those who follow them will attract less. Those who wander about without any sense of direction will attract nothing. Life is not fair and wealth does not distribute itself equally. Those who have the knowledge will always have the advantage.

As government participates in the tension between those who create wealth and those who do not, it sets itself up for failure as well. Since government does not create anything, except regulations and protections, its intrusion into the private sector economy will always yield increased tensions and tend to reward failure and penalize success. The best thing government can do for the economy is to stay as far away from it as possible, while providing for safety and protection from criminal activity.

Every person on the face of the planet shares something in common. We are all given a mind that we use to learn, dream, think, relate, love, fear, and so forth. All human emotions and human thoughts come to us through the mind. It is the use of this wonderful asset that determines our status in life and the rewards that we receive, or don't, as the case may be.

Not all minds are equal. Some seem to be driven to self destruction while others are humming away in building great inventive structures and products. Everything starts with a thought. The end result of wealth begins with how we use the mind. No one comes into the world with assets ascribed to them. Some come into families who have wealth, but in our raw and first born state, we are devoid of anything that we have created or earned. From that point on, the difference in our station in life is determined by how we use the mind to accumulate information and put it into productive use. If we are wise, we as a culture will encourage that process and not penalize it by taking from it the rewards that inevitably flow to it.

Resentment of the wealth of others will not make you more productive or competitive in this thing called life. It will only sap the time and strength you could otherwise use to enter the stream of creativity and to produce what your mind is capable of thinking about. The development of the mind is the development of wealth for wealth flows toward power and knowledge is power.

Wealth, in this sense transcends money. Money is only representative of value. It has no intrinsic value in the paper and ink contained therein. The value is in the asset that is represented by the money. When knowledge and creativity are developed, the natural course of reward is represented by money. Money is not, in this sense, the asset itself. There is an elusive trend in our world to think of the productive as greedy, money hungry hoarders of wealth that should be equally distributed. But seldom are the creative interested in the end result. They are most often driven to create and to accomplish and the money is simply the end result. Greed, in this sense, belongs to those who resent wealth and who do not understand the direct connection between creating and rewards. Resentment of wealth is a waste of time and will not get you wealth at all. It will only get you an ulcer.

The accumulation of information and the use of it is the key to asset value in our world today.

Chapter Fifteen

The Power of Personality

For many years now, our family has been playing a little game. When we go places and do things, we automatically survey the room or setting to find the power personality. Many years ago there was a speaker who frequented our church who was a power personality. When he came into the room, he took up half the space and breathed up most of the oxygen. He did not know this about himself, nor did he try to create it. It just happened. All eyes shifted toward him when he came into the room.

For more than 50 years we have been involved in the world of pure bred dogs, breeding, raising, training and showing German Shepherd Dogs. On the show circuit there is a power person. He is a professional handler and travels from show to show, and is heavily involved in the culture and relationships of that world.

After one of the shows, we went to an 'after the show party.' I told my daughter to time the crowd response from the time this person arrived at the party until there was a circle of chairs around him, listening to him. I predicted it would take no more than five minutes. We both saw him come into the room, get his plate of refreshments and go find an empty chair. Within five minutes, there was a semicircle of people around him, facing his chair and, listening intently to his stories and opinions. He does not know this about himself. He thinks he is just one of the crowd but everyone else knows he is a power person. He rules the social setting simply because of his personality.

There are courses given to organize the attributes of leadership, but what we are talking about here is different from leadership. Leadership is conveyed by responsibility and one's role in the organization. The power personality can be anywhere in the structure and will still have power, simply because. It is also evident in animals. We had a female German Shepherd Dog some years ago who ruled the house simply by her stare. She said nothing, demanded nothing, but all the dogs watched her for direction.

We are all genetically different and have personalities that are different. What constitutes the component parts of personality is a consideration explored by social scientists and psychologists, but I have not seen a study that analyzes the component parts of the power personality. It is difficult to define, but unmistakable when present.

This attribute, this sense of power given to a person because of their personality, plays a large role in human success and in the accumulation of wealth. Some people are just pleasant and easy to be around. They are likable. Some are not. Some people seem to rile those around them without doing a thing. Defining those nuances of personality is at least difficult if not downright impossible, yet they determine a person's role in life. We can work to learn how to find our 'right' place in the social strata of human interaction, but to some degree, we are given a personality and we are stuck with it. If we decide it is not fair, that we are unattractive and without certain social sensitivities, then we will spend our lives in regret and envy. To be able to accept ourselves and then work to improve our knowledge and understanding is the task of every person. The height to which we rise will be determined by the degree to which we are able to make progress in our world, with our given genetics and personality.

For those who are simply born with a sense of power about them, few know they are that 'kind of person.' It is not learned, it just is. Because of this phenomenon, having power limitations in the political arena is essential. The separation of powers was understood and prescribed by our founding fathers to keep strong and attractive personalities from exercising power over others that they should not have. The essence of personal power is that everyone should be responsible for themselves and everyone should be free from the intrusion of others into their arena of responsibility. Every level of power has limits. The problem is, not all kinds of power are easy to define and to resist.

Some people seem unable to stand up to other people who accumulate power. Some people cannot seem to speak up when there needs to be a clear voice of reason. Some people will allow bondage for the sake of peace, but the ultimate result of capitulation is not peace. Slavery is the result. For every personality, there is the responsibility to be aware of other people and not overstep their responsibility for themselves. Everyone has to make their own decisions if freedom is to be truly free and liberty to be meaningful.

Being intimidated by the powerful is the seed plot of bondage. Regardless of their position or their personality type, no one can stand over us and assume superiority unless we allow it. It is our responsibility to be able to read the power structures, and the power people, in our world and to negotiate our own way through them.

Chapter Sixteen

The Power of Culture

She was a reasonably attractive young lady with a pleasing personality. She was the administrator of an American Indian Tribe and was in trouble. She confessed that she'd tried everything to do things right and had studied the rules and procedures manuals fervently to make sure she was doing things right. But alas, she was in trouble and was about to be fired. She looked up at me with tears in her eyes and asked what she had done wrong.

I explained that every people group and culture has rules, procedures and expectations. The problem is only one third of them are codified. They are like an iceberg with the visual part codified in books and sitting on the shelves. The assumption is, those are the rules and those are the measuring devices for our performance. But there is more. Under the waterline are the other two thirds of the iceberg. This is the cultural history, the unwritten and even unknown rules of the group. If asked about them, there may be a denial that they exist but be assured, they exist. They will never be used in a formal charge of violation of the rules, but they will work to find a violation that might be overlooked without the violation of the cultural expectations.

For the insider, those cultural points below the waterline are understood, even though they may not be any better able to define them than the violator can. For the outsider, who has not grown up in the culture, it is impossible to know what those rules and expectations are. You only know when you have offended someone who knows that you simply do not do things that way.

With that explanation the young tribal administrator smiled, acknowledged that she finally understood the phenomenon of her being fired, and was able to blame it on the unspoken nuances of the culture rather than on personal failure.

My grandfather came to America from Germany as a young man. He married, and started to raise a family. He had certain rules about this transition that were important to him. He did not allow the family to speak German, simply because it was not the language of the new culture he was trying to be assimilated into. He would not allow his family to live in a segregated part of a community. He made it clear that he had come to America to become an American and he would not allow himself or his family to remain 'under the waterline.' He made friends of people of various ethnic backgrounds and cultivated friendships with those who had been here and who understood those cultural imperatives that were unspoken, unknown, unwritten and below the waterline.

When one remains culturally separate from the mainstream of any group, or within any nation, they separate themselves from both power and wealth. They fail to understand the true nature of the power structure and the cultural bastions of power. Some, separated by this lack of cultural understanding, try to garner support for their separate culture within the culture. The end result is that the main culture is a power base, in and of itself, and the power of the culture is not shared freely with those who are outside.

Many years ago, we had a church meeting and various members were standing to give their opinion on an issue. Finally, a nice looking man in business attire rose and offered an opinion. There was silence. The silence spoke of the suspicion the regular members had of this outsider. He had not earned the right to speak. After several moments of silence he rose once again and said, "Hi! My name is Bill Anderson and I like this church and I am going to be a part of it, and unless you tar and feather me, I'm going to find acceptance from you. And you know what; you're going to love me." Everyone laughed and the atmosphere changed and he was accepted and yes, we did love him.

It is incumbent on those who come into the group or culture to make their way past the unspoken and unknown rules and earn their right to be a part. We often think it is the responsibility of the group to be nice to the visitor and invite them in, and that is certainly admirable. But there is another side to that dilemma. Those who come in, and do not know the rules, will be judged and accepted by them whether they are written and known or not. There is always the culture beneath the waterline.

America is a culture. It has rules and a history. It has principles on which it is founded. It has laws by which we administer limits and expectations. But it also has the subtle unknowns that one has to find and fit into. Our fascination with multi-culturalism may have done us a disservice in allowing people to bring their culture with them and thus avoid understanding the history and principles that define the mainstream culture of America. Without this submission to the total iceberg of the culture, people are left at odds with the overall sense of what America is all about.

It is not a matter of forcing everyone to conform to a rigid expectation of order. It is more an invitation to them to reach beyond what they have been to embrace what they can be. Unless we extend to them both the formal legal precepts of our nation and the hidden implications of our history and founding principles, we do a disservice to both the one trying to find a way in and those who have. It is not a matter of conformity but of inclusion within the informal relationships of the culture. We have been really good at honoring other cultures. We may have been really lacking in allowing those who come to struggle to earn their way into the greater sense of national identity.

When that inclusion has not happened, we have, by the very nature of culture and how power flows, left those who come in from other cultures, outside of the power and the flow of wealth. The flow of wealth is a relational thing. It is not determined by legal dictate nor by governmental fiat. It is relational. People do business with and work for those whom they know, trust, and who share their cultural expectations. To not fit into that greater culture is to choose to be isolated from power and wealth. Because it is a cultural issue, it is rectified by making a determination to be a part of the culture we want to fit into. Once we make that choice, we will live with the level of power and advantage that is present in the culture we have chosen.

Chapter Seventeen

The Power of Need

Necessity is the mother of invention, we are told, yet we constantly want to avoid necessity. Odd, we humans! I remember starting out on our annual vacation trip to the Sierras as a child. Dad would hitch up the luggage trailer he built. It was complete with side boards that served as tables and a canvas covering that served as a tarp cover while traveling, then was propped up with poles to make the trailer into a sleeping tent.

Camping was our thing and getting there was half the fun. Dad always took along a tool kit, a roll of wire, an extra fan belt and two spare tires. Those were the days. They don't make cars like they used to, or tires, as a matter of fact, and that is a good thing. We knew that somewhere on our journey there would be at least one blow out and then we would set about to pry the old tire off the rim and put in a new tube, then hook the old tire pump up and pump away until it was properly inflated. The wire? Oh it had many uses when the car broke down. Dad was the master of inventiveness when it came to the old car, so when it broke Dad would look and think and figure something out and then we'd be on our way again.

Life is easier now. Cars simply do not break down like they used to and they last far longer than ever before. Tires? We used to get about 15,000 miles to a tire in those days, where now it is common to get 50,000-60,000 miles. Yes times have changed and in terms of technology and mechanical things, it has changed for the better.

But there was something about those olden days that was good for us. It was man against machine and the task was to be smarter than the car, or washing machine or whatever it was that broke. Things were not disposable then and figuring out how to fix them was both a necessity and the game of testosterone versus apparatus. To win out over those adversaries of broken things was part of the mystique of being a man and being alive.

It was also the crucible of inventiveness. You could not just replace the machine, you had to fix it and for most rural people, fixing it yourself was part of the daily task. It was also the task of the soldiers sent away to the great wars of our past. They were given the weapons and the rations and were expected to improvise along the way. You could not grab your cell phone and call customer support. You were on your own. No one was on the battlefield to take care of your weapon for you and no one was there to do your laundry, fix your meals or fix the broken jeep. You could fix things and move on or sit there and wait for the enemy to come and get you. Necessity was a common companion and a constant pressure.

Yes, things have changed. Today we replace things, throw them away, and think in modular terms when repairs are possible. The electronic circuitry in most modern machines and gadgets makes it possible to just unplug the faulty module and plug in a new one. You do not have to dig into it to find the error; you just throw the module away and plug in a new one.

With this change in mindset we have gained a lot, but possibly we have lost something also. We have lost the sense of self sufficiency that required us to learn about the things we used and how they worked and how to make them work again. We have lost the sense of necessity that gives rise to the inventiveness that drives us forward. We have learned to rely on government programs to take care of us and to expect the structures of society to support our care and eliminate our needs. We have come to expect that someone, somewhere will take care of it, whatever it is! Someone is in charge of changing the light bulb - oh, excuse me - we do not have light bulbs anymore. Well, someone will change the light tube or pick up the trash or deal with the crime or see that everyone is fed or...

As I write, there are massive demonstrations across our land by those who resent the wealthy and the productive. They are picketing Wall Street in an effort to make the wealthy and productive feel guilty so they will spread the wealth around. Some of the cities where the demonstrations are taking place are supportive, providing fire wood, tents and sleeping accommodations for the demonstrators. The effect is to underscore the message that we do not want these dissidents to have to take care of themselves while they are making their statement against those who do. We have become a spoiled, lazy and mentally inept generation who abhor necessity and demand to be taken care of.

One of the primary tenets of Al-Anon is, support success, do not support failure. It may seem harsh, but it works. As long as you do for the child what he should do for himself, he will continue allowing you to do so. But if you teach children to do for themselves and then refuse to do it for them, they will learn to take responsibility for themselves. If you keep covering for the alcoholic and picking up the pieces of their lives, they will never change.

Years ago I walked into a supermarket to pick up a few things and there in the center isle was a little boy, throwing a tantrum. He was down on the floor crying, kicking and screaming at the top of his lungs. The mother was beside herself with embarrassment, trying to pick him up, move him along, and was giving him her 30th last warning. I watched for a moment as she would glance my way in an apologetic manner and then try again to get him to cooperate. Finally, I walked up beside her and explained that I was a minister and counselor and possibly I could help. She started crying and offered that she had no idea what to do. He did it all the time when they went shopping and, yes, she would appreciate some help. So, I briefly explained he was getting the attention he wanted and bargaining with her for what he wanted. I explained that the only way to stop this behavior was to take away his power. Then I told her to stop talking to him, stop trying to get his attention and quit making threats. I told her - no more last warnings, just turn around, walk away, go out of the store and get in her car. I told her I would make sure he was safe.

She paused for a moment, looked me up and down, then in utter frustration, did as I had instructed. As soon as she was out of sight the little fellow saw he had lost his audience so the drama ceased. He realized he was alone, so he sprang to his feet and ran to find his mother. She barely got to the car before he was at her side. We talked and she asked if I had this kind of problems with my children. I explained we did not. She wanted to know why. I explained we do not give repeated warnings of impending consequences that never come. We give one instruction, then action. No warnings. No counting to three. No doing for them what they must learn to do for themselves.

Love is not permissive, but neither is it harsh. It instructs, helps, teaches and then allows for trial and error in the learning curve. But the end result is to not take care of the need for the needy as they learn to take care of it themselves. Love sees beyond the immediate need to the self-sufficiency that is best for the one loved. It all comes back to the proposition that if you give a man a fish, you have fed him for the day, but if you teach him to fish you have solved his need for a lifetime.

Our socialistic political bent is like the mother in the market. The needy are throwing a tantrum and the government is thrashing about to determine who caused it, how to stop it and who is going to take care of it. The answer, more often than not, is to turn and walk away. Necessity is the mother of invention. Most people are capable of getting up off of the floor, drying their eyes and getting on with life. To not allow them the pain of making that transition is the greater evil of government. Need is good for us. It is the crucible of learning, of growing and of becoming self sufficient, and with self sufficiency comes power - to create, to produce and to be alive.

Chapter Eighteen

The Power of Religion

Matthew 22:15 Then the Pharisees went out and laid plans to trap him in his words. 16 They sent their disciples to him along with the Herodians. "Teacher," they said, "we know that you are a man of integrity and that you teach the way of God in accordance with the truth. You aren't swayed by others, because you pay no attention to who they are. 17 Tell us then, what is your opinion? Is it right to pay the imperial tax[a] to Caesar or not?" 18 But Jesus, knowing their evil intent, said, "You hypocrites, why are you trying to trap me? 19 Show me the coin used for paying the tax." They brought him a denarius, 20 and he asked them, "Whose image is this? And whose inscription?" 21 "Caesar's," they replied. Then he said to them, "So give back to Caesar what is Caesar's, and to God what is God's." 22 When they heard this, they were amazed. So they left him and went away.

The profile of Jesus' life revealed a radical departure from the traditions of the past. He violated sabbatical law, ate and drank with sinners and tax collectors, did not get along well with the religious sorts of the synagogue and advanced what may well be the most radical teaching of God's government.

Government and the process of political control has always been a difficult matter for the human race. Most societies in history were ruled by the authority of the toughest guy around. The general political theory was that might makes right. The ruling point of power was most often the one with the biggest gun. It seems, for the most part little has changed. Most cultures are still ruled by either a person or a group who have the power and the wealth.

It was out of that dilemma that Jesus was approached by the Pharisees. They were ruled over by the Roman Empire and were thrashing under its abrasive authority. They were looking for a champion to rid them of that tyranny and with the popularity of Jesus in His early ministry, were hoping that he might be the one. But alas, he disappointed them and seemed to refuse to rise to the occasion or to the political issues of their agenda.

When they came to trap him and to make him declare his intentions and his political stance, he advanced, not a quest for political power, but a theory that cut across their entire worldview. He spoke of two kingdoms. He advanced the theory that the Kingdom of God was a spiritual kingdom and operated outside of the arena of secular governmental rule. But, he refused also to contrast it with the Kingdom of Man and the secular authority of Rome. He blew their minds, transcending the dichotomy they had in their world view. They were predisposed to accept one government and one alone. Jesus advanced the theory that human government can exist in parallel with spiritual government and that the two can exist in the same geography without contrast. He refused to buy into the contrast and thus ignited a concept that was little understood in history and is still difficult for people to understand.

The founders of this great nation we enjoy today understood that principle and provided that the state would neither restrict nor create a religion, leaving faith as a matter for the church and the conscience of those who gathered for spiritual fellowship and spiritual government. They provided room for the church to exist in parallel with the state and to both operate without interference from the other. But they did not, as some have come to believe, want to wall off the church from the affairs of human government or to leave the church free to compete for power against the state. There was recognition of separate arenas of power and that their coexistence was not a threat to the other.

Unfortunately, many see the power of the church and its influence as a threat and believe that those who attend church should not be involved in the affairs of state. Nonsense! It was not the teaching of Jesus that we should select either the power of the church or the power of the state but that both were God ordained to coexist together.

I remember the furor that arose many years ago when John F. Kennedy was elected President. There was great fear in many circles because of his religion - he was a Catholic. The fear was that his religion would get in the way of his politics and that a person of his religious convictions should not be president.

This issue has arisen periodically in our country and it is again an issue in this election cycle. There are those who propose that anyone who is blatantly religious should not be elected for the same reason - their religion will get in the way of their political decisions and bottom line, we cannot trust them. This, for those who espouse it, is the separation of church and state. Religious people should not hold public office, they say.

For me, the issue is quite different. A person who is anti-religion should not hold office. Let me define that a bit. I do not consider myself a religious person in that religion, by definition, is the systems and cultures that are created to approach God and to please Him. Since I am firmly committed to Christianity as a relationship, not a religion, I believe I am accepted by God and that I do not have to work my way into God's favor, be a part of the right denomination, or even have the right doctrinal statement - as though I could know enough to claim to have all truth. A relationship with God removes all of that human arrogance and measures us, not by our ability to get to God, but accepts that He has provided a means by which He comes to us - (An opposite way of thinking from religion, per se). I am accepted and do not need to prove it!

The problem is with our Constitution and the Bill of Rights which affirms that we are endowed by our Creator with certain unalienable rights. The reason for this premise is because of the history behind our founding fathers. They were breaking away from the historic governmental system of monarchies which held the premise that all power and all rights were in the king and the king could do no wrong. The foundations of this nation were to prohibit government from intruding into the private lives and private property of the people. So, we affirm that those rights are not conveyed by the government but by God Himself and that no government has the right to enter that territory.

So, if a person affirms there is no God, then they are at cross purposes with the premise of our founding documents and are predisposed to believe our rights, although attributed to God, are really just flowery language from some demented concepts of our founding fathers and are not really true. They therefore must conclude, absent a God who granted these rights, that they are, in fact given by government, even though the founding documents do not say so, and thus are subject to government changing its mind. This all relates to our concept of the Constitution and our founding documents. If the Constitution is a living document and subject to change, then so are our rights to personal space and personal property. We can change the documents and also change the rights they protect. Many, possibly most, of our governmental officials today, believe that it can and should be changed.

Against that position are those like myself who are strict constitutionalists. We believe that those guarantees in our founding documents are there to restrict the power of government and should remain as written. This restricts the courts from making legislation and focuses their power on reviewing law and public actions in the light of the Constitution - plus nothing.

So, I believe that a person in public office should be able to affirm that the Creator gave us our rights and that government is limited by that act of God Himself.

Secondly, there is the issue of the candidate who is religious but whose religion I do not agree with or understand. What should we do with such a person and should we vote for them?

In our scriptural text above, Jesus deals with this very question. He advances a concept that is spoken to in the Old Testament to some degree, but is clearly articulated in this event in the life of Jesus. He proposes two kingdoms - The Kingdom of God and the Kingdom of Man. He makes a distinction between powers and the kind of authority that exists in the economy of the Creator God. That is, God has given two forms of authority into our world. Both are from God and both are to be honored. Spiritual authority is given to the church while civil authority is given to human government. Human government operates in the arena of the law, which is the instrument of limiting the behavior of the evil and the lawless. It is a means of self preservation for human governments and nations and is to be honored.

The Apostle Paul writes the powers that be are ordained by God to bring fear to the lawless. Soldiers and police officers are thus ordained by God to keep us safe. The church, conversely, deals with spiritual issues and influences. While civil government is the instrument of the law, the church is to be the instrument of God's grace in bringing spiritual conversion to the people, so that the nature of Christ inside does not need the external policeman outside. Where morality and ethics are concerned, there are overlapping areas, but in the greater sense, both civil government and the church should live in harmony with distinct arenas of power and without conflict.

It is in recognition of the two kingdoms that our founding fathers provided for the separation of powers, not only in the halls of government but in the right to the freedom of religion. Note, it is not freedom from religion, but the freedom of religion. Rightly understood, there is no conflict. Thus those who serve in government are free to enter the halls of the church without conflict and participate in their faith and not be a threat to the government. Similarly, people of faith have the right to enter the halls of government and to serve or petition or influence without there being a conflict.

There is a problem however. For there are politically motivated people who want to restrict the presence and influence of people of faith into the halls of government. And there are religious people who do not understand or hold to the separation of powers of two kingdoms. They hold that God has only authorized the church to hold power and to rule in the name of God. Both of those extremes are a danger to our society.

Let me speak specifically...

I listened to a talk show the other night and a caller stated that they could not support a candidate because he was Mormon. Another called and could not support another candidate because she had written boldly about her Christian faith. I disagreed. Since my grandfather was a devout Mormon Bishop and my mother was raised Mormon, I thought I understood a bit about the situation. I am not Mormon and disagree with the Mormon statement of faith. But I do understand they hold to the separation of powers of the church and civil government, so I would not be looking at the candidates' religious faith but their political policies and history to determine if I would support them in that arena.

Most of the presidents in our past would not pass muster theologically if I were the judge of their faith. But I am not, and they have not asked for my opinion. My vote for public office has a different criterion than my fellowship in my church. I accept that there are two kingdoms.

On the other side of this issue are those who hold to religions that will not accept civil government and who want to superimpose their laws and traditions over the authority of our government. One example is the Muslim faith that centralizes all power in the Imam and the traditions and laws of the church. Their objective is to make disciples to the religion, by force if necessary and to elevate the systems and law of their faith over and above that of civil government. To do so would eradicate our God given rights and make them subject to human control. This should never happen and should be resisted at all cost.

So, while I would vote for someone of a different faith, if their political views were right, I would not vote for someone who holds to a faith that centralizes the power of the government under religious law. This, I believe, is not the position of Christianity, Judaism and many other religions and is not in the best interest of our country or its private citizens.

The church and the government can coexist together quite well and Moses, Jesus and our forefathers agreed. Let's try not to mess it up from here on.

How Power Operates

1. Power tends to accumulate

Some people love power. Power is addictive. Some people accumulate power, love it and, are addicted to it, and they require more and more to get the same effect. This is the evil that our forefathers foresaw in placing limits on power in our government.

The accumulation of power in government will bring an end to that government. The inevitable end of the accumulation of power is the loss of power all together. There are two extremes: A weak government with no power that is chaotic, and a government that has accumulated all power, which is equally chaotic.

When a government becomes so large and so intrusive in vain attempts to care for all things, and when the extraction of payment to maintain such a government is impossible to maintain, the government and the economy will collapse, not leaving control and a nanny state, but chaos.

The opposite extreme, or no government, is chaos. The extreme of too much government is also chaos. The continuum of these extremes is not a flat line going to different extremes, but circular, where the extremes meet at the extension of those extremes. Too much or too little ends up at the same point.

Power in all cases must be limited to the defined responsibilities of the Constitution, the job description, or the role one has in relationship to others. The wise leader will use power to empower others and to lift them to a higher level, personally, economically and socially. Lifting others never diminishes the one doing the lifting. In fact, it enhances their role and creates a flow of power through them as it is given away freely.

But the common way of dealing with the powerless is to take from those who have the power and the wealth and to give it by legal fiat to those who have not. The problem is unless those who have not are elevated internally by education, experience, value, creativity and responsibility, receiving the wealth and power of others will not benefit them. They will squander it on the immediate and remain at the same level of living. We cannot help the poor and the ignorant by taking care of them. We only really help them by giving them the skills and abilities that are essential to hold the power they are given.

2. Power tends to corrupt

As we have said earlier, power is essential to the function of a point of responsibility, but where it exceeds the responsibility, it is abuse. It does not become abuse, it is abuse. The abuse of power at any level will corrupt the holder of that power. Primarily we have focused on the abuse of political power, but anywhere power exists, and it exists everywhere in everyone, it can be abusive and corrupting when it is not limited by the responsibility given.

We have all experienced the arrogant person who believes their own press and assumes that because of their position, knowledge, personality, looks or whatever attribute they hold, they are simply better than the rest of us and have privileges that we do not have. The privilege of power is easily seen in the scandals in religion, politics, business and in everyday life. This arrogance seems to attach itself to those who, for whatever reason, make the subtle, even if unknown assumption that they have the right to be above and to rule over those who are, at least constitutionally, their equal.

"We hold these truths to be self evident, that all men are created equal..." This bold statement flies in the face of millennia of class distinctions, the privilege of position and of the Divine Right of Kings. Certainly it is not a quantitative statement, for none of us are the same. We are different in size, shape, genetic structure, intelligence, skill, aptitude, and any category we can name. Life is not fair and equality is more than the end result of being born into this world. Many different factors go into the making of a life and the end result is inequality of wealth, position and power. So we have to understand the equality that is being advanced by our founding fathers is something more or something less than our being equal in or sameness of persona. What that statement conveys is that we are equal in the rights that have been granted by our Creator. By virtue of that equality, we deserve the same respect and consideration when it comes to being human, existing on this planet and having access to the opportunities that are presented to all of humanity.

3. Control demeans

No one has the right to presume that they can or should choose for us our course in life or determine for us how we should exercise our freedoms under law. There is no politician wise enough to tell us how to live our life or what choices we should make. There is no preacher smart enough to take from us the power of choice or the freedom that is innately ours. Guidance is one thing, control is quite another.

The problem with excess power is that it presumes the right to control. Freedom, by its simplest definition, is the lack of constraint and control. The nature of excess power is to presume that we, by virtue of our superiority, should correct those who are less gifted, less educated or less organized so they can have the benefits of our paternalism. In government it is the accumulation of laws, rules and regulations until every area of life and human action is determined by superior leaders who know best. In families, it is the inability of the parent to guide and educate and then to release. In the business it is the boss who micromanages to the point the employees' presence is unnecessary because the boss is unable to release the tasks to the employee. In all of life, excess power spills over as control.

Control is the enemy of personal growth, of personal productivity and of inventiveness. Control raids the freedom of another for the sake of pillaging power from them. Control is both arrogant and ignorant. It cannot see the value or genius in another but presumes superiority and thus the need to be over, to be the head and to control.

But, all that is the apparent side of the controlling personality. For underneath the apparent arrogance is fear. Yes, fear! Fear that, if I do not control things and people I will be exposed for the average human that I am. The corporate side of fear is that if I do not control the people around me they will go astray. However, that assumption obscures the possibility that if I release people and provide them with freedom, they will excel, grow and become better. An overpowering government does not believe in the value, worth and competence of its people. If it did, it would not do for them what they can do for themselves. Control is demeaning, creates dependence and stifles the potential of humanity.

Freedom allows people to become their best, while control believes people are incapable of becoming better. Freedom makes room for failure and another try while control removes the possibility of failure by reducing that possibility. When risk is reduced, so is potential. Risk is an essential ingredient in the path to success.

4. Control changes our perceptions

Psychological studies of power and its influence on us repeatedly conclude that the more power one has over others and the more we recognize the privilege that power brings, the more we tend to think differently about ourselves and other people. Humility and power are seldom bedfellows. The more power one has, the more they tend to believe it is earned and owned. Power, in a sense then, creates the assurance that it is deserved.

At the same time, the more power one has the more we tend to ignore advice from below us, indicating that we begin to believe we are in power because we know better and that those below us are inferior to us. This is almost a universal trait. Few people in power are able to separate themselves from the position they hold. The assumption is that we have arrived at a higher level of power because we deserve it. Arrogance is the end result of the corrupting influence of power.

Then what of confidence? Is not confidence an admirable and desirable trait? Certainly this is true. But there is a difference between being confident of one's self and of the abilities one has to perform the responsibilities given and using that power position in comparison to others. Confidence in one's self does not require demeaning others. Confidence and humility are allies in the legitimate use of power within the scope of our responsibility. That is, to be effective in handling a position of power, one does not have to look down on others.

Without understanding this phenomenon, we will probably be corrupted by power. With understanding, we can avoid the trap and refuse to think of ourselves as superior simply because we attain a greater level of success. The test of success is one of the most difficult in the human experience.

Chapter Twenty

Power Allegiances

While I affirm that power is not evil and is essential to the handling of responsibility, I also affirm that power can take on a life of its own and bring illegitimate control if allowed to do so. In this thought, there are two factors to be considered:

- Illegitimate control

- Allowing illegitimate control

The accumulation of power is one thing, but there is another layer of this phenomenon – the allegiances that power makes in protecting itself. If the accumulation of power results in war or in competition or in some other form of 'face off,' then its strength is dissipated in the protecting of itself against its enemy. But very often, power bases, rather than confronting their competition as an enemy, join forces in allegiances of power. That allegiance can be the formation of alliances between nations, the formation of trade partnerships between nations, the consolidation of companies, who form strategic agreements to share capital control, or any number of consortiums of power.

The above examples of accumulation of power are not necessarily illegitimate or evil in and of themselves. But to the degree that people and markets are controlled, and regulations stifle the entrance of others into the arena of productivity, then, this power can be evil when it results in illegitimately and unnaturally fencing off itself to the exclusion of others.

I want to walk carefully here, for some companies have grown large and by the sheer momentum of their creativity have dominated markets. When they grow and create, they are also creating jobs, stimulating creativity and growing the economy, so in this, they can hardly be considered evil in the greater sense. This is part of the free market system even though it does create a barrier to competition from the small entrepreneur who is trying to get into the market. One can get into the market by doing something better or having a better idea, but without capitalization to support such a move, the big guy who has already paid his dues and won the market does have a distinct advantage.

Again, there is nothing evil in economic power, personal power or the accumulation of power. But it tends to erode the greater realities of life when it creates the inevitable arrogance to which we fallible humans are vulnerable. When anyone, either individually or corporately begins to think of themselves, their enterprise, or their wealth as a stamp of significance and a badge of superiority, then evil is present. When the politician rules because they believe they are better than or more capable of deciding for the ignorant what is best for them, then evil exists. When the corporate structure so stifles the life of the component part that it has no significance and no value beyond its hourly contribution, then evil exists.

The financial allegiances of Venice, from 1275 through 1350 controlled and dominated a huge international "bubble" of currency, which collapsed in the 1340's. The mutual greed of the bankers of Florence and the merchants of Venice bankrupted them and the economies of Europe and the Mediterranean. The problem was not in their successful accumulation of wealth but in forgetting those who contributed to that wealth and in seeking an advantage at the expense of a sense of fairness in the market. The problem was created, not by the government of Venice, the city state itself, but when it allowed the control of the currency by the allegiance of bankers who dominated commerce and when it set unreasonable tariffs, taxes, fees and exchange rates, thus accumulating wealth at the expense of the rest of the world. It was the accumulation of wealth at one place (the bubble) that created the downfall.

This is not the only example of power accumulating and ultimately consuming itself. It happens periodically in human history. We seem to wander through periods of famine and want, rise to see productivity and wealth, then fall again into the imbalance of access to wealth. The issue is not the power to produce, but the accumulation of that power in exclusive echelons of allegiances of power that shut off the flow of personal power and the rights of the people at any level to have the freedom to produce, grow and create. Whether it is caused by government control or private corporate control, the effect is the same.

It happens simply. The dollar, or any national unit of currency, has a certain value, but that value is not really certain, for it is assigned. Someone says how much that unit of currency is worth. In our current economic system our Federal Reserve, by its influence on our system, makes that determination. Our free economy also influences that value by the ongoing exchange of goods and services between a willing buyer and a willing seller, affirming that we trust that value.

But all systems are not equal. Right now we are facing a balance of trade problem with Mainland China in that the government of China determines the value of their currency and keeps it artificially low. The end result is that they are accumulating value and creating debt for our nation and other nations who buy their goods and services.

The reality is, a piece of paper with fancy formal inscriptions of value on it is, in reality worth nothing more than the value of the paper it is printed on and the ink that makes the inscriptions. Its representative value is not in the paper note itself but in the value assigned to it. That value is determined by those in power. In Venice it was the bankers who assigned value. In our system it is the Federal Reserve, the control assigned to it by our government and the influence of the market. In China it is the government alone. The end result is that value systems are not always in agreement as to the value of our money internationally.

What occurs then is an inequality of power and a struggle for power from competing power bases to have control of the currency and to determine its value. There are also false measures of value that influence our economy. The rise in popularity of the derivatives market in our economy is a great illustration. Derivatives are simply the selling of debt as an asset to investors. In the 1990's we had a great upward trend of mortgage debt and many investors got into it, buying up that debt as an investment. The theory is simple: When the debt is paid back, plus the interest, it is worth more than its face value. But, with these mortgages, in many cases, they were worthless. Their assigned value was inflated by illusions of their worth. Ultimately, they were only as good as the ability of the people who made the debt to repay that debt. As the inflated prices of houses and the economy began to adjust, the mortgage on the house was sometimes more than double the value of the house. Construction stopped, jobs were lost, payment could no longer be made and the entire bubble popped. Banks and investors were left with their derivative investments which had a face value of 'X' amount, but which could not be sold for even half the assigned value.

What is the value of the dollar? It is only as valuable as the foundations of the economy around it allow it to be. It doesn't matter who says what it is worth, it only matters what you can buy with it. In a depression, the man with the bag of food is king, while the man with the bag of gold is begging. The point is the accumulation of power over wealth and the allegiances of power and the ability to assign value is of little worth if the economy surrounding you is not able to respond to the value assigned.

That is why the accumulation of power must always be limited by the power of the individual. If we lose the power of a representative republic, we lose the power of the economy. The egis of control must always be in the hands of "we the people." We determine who is elected. We determine which products sell and which corporations garner economic power. We determine which banks hold our investments and our assets. We make those determinations, and if we allow the power of corporate interests or government dictates to gain control over us, we must blame ourselves and fight to regain the control we lose.

We have passed through a period of time when career politicians have learned how to manipulate the system and to use their accumulated power to control trends, markets, outcomes and to partner with banking and corporate interests to direct the flow of value and power.

One of the ways we keep this from happening is through term limits. Our government started as a group of concerned volunteers, serving for the good of the nation. It has become a monster of controls, bureaus and regulations, increasingly determining what water we will drink, what light bulbs we will buy, what food we will consume and whether or not our dog can have puppies. The argument against term limits is that we will then turn out those leaders who are the most valuable and who have learned how to use the system to our advantage. Yes, that is exactly the point. When we depend on the government to do for us what we should do for ourselves, then it is too big, too powerful and too intrusive. The more we allow government to do for us, the more personal power we lose. That continuum is absolute. If you give away power, it is gone and will not always be used as you would use it. The only way to keep that from happening is to not give it away. We do that by not voting for the person who promises to do the most for us but by voting for the person who promises to do the least. While the protection of the nation and the maintaining of the armies in readiness is the primary function of government, everything else must be rationed carefully by the people to its government or it will accumulate power to the point that we will need permission to flush our toilets. Oh... wait a minute... We already do, at least in terms of how much water we use to do so.

Any use of power and particularly the allegiances of power, to be successful, have to maintain the proper sense of direction of their power. It is not theirs by right, by dictate or by personal superiority. It is theirs because it is given by the people, the customer and the employee. In a sense then, their greatest objective in the pursuit of profit is not the power of the profit only, but the welfare of their source of power: The people!

Corporations without customers are without power. Power is not something that is theirs to give away or to use to control. It is theirs because it is given by the people who purchase their products. The products are for sale because of the people who work for them and produce those products. The wise company will always keep this power relationship in mind and understand that they are in business at the will and by the approval of their people, both customers and employees. Their highest corporate objective then is servicing the needs of their people base, without which there is no company and no profit.

Chapter Twenty One

The Murder of Beethoven

I shall never forget the scene, now many years ago, but always fresh. I was going into our local supermarket for some things and so were a mother and her four to five year old child. As I was walking near their car, they got out whereupon the mother immediately grabbed the child and scolded him soundly. She told him how awful he always behaved when they came to the store and how she was not going to put up with it any longer. She shook him soundly, told him how bad he was and what she was going to do to him if he acted the same way he always acted when they went shopping. She angrily reduced the child to tears and a defiant sneer as she jerked him toward the store entrance.

I stopped, taken back by the loud and angry scene and tried to get my wits about me again. Then I heard a still small voice inside me saying, "You just witnessed the murder of Beethoven."

I have always believed that in every human being is the spark of genius, waiting to be discovered, cultivated, developed and released. But I had witnessed what was obviously an ongoing power struggle in which the circle of violence was killing any chance this child or the mother had of personal fulfillment. Whatever the Beethoven was in this child was already severely damaged and approaching death. In an effort to control and retain power, this parent had no idea how to encourage the spark of genius waiting to be discovered and released.

This phenomenon is not novel or new. It has gone on as long as the human family has been alive. Parents, without knowing what they are doing, very often provide more damage to their children than they do support and empowerment. I was fortunate to have been born into a loving traditional family and do not ever remember not feeling loved. My parents thought I was special as they did my sisters. Their expectations followed us and hounded us to explore life and to find our strengths and to develop them. As I look around our world, I realize that our family was not typical, but exceptional.

The other day our 6 year old grandson got up early, made breakfast and then made coffee for his dad and brought him a cup, with the right amount of sugar and cream. He had been watching and knew how dad made his coffee. His dad was taken by his thoughtfulness and the precision with which he did these chores and asked him why he had, all of a sudden, taken it on himself to do this. His answer melted dad's heart and started a chain of bragging through the family. He simply said, "I just want to be a good boy!"

Here was further evidence that a young man who is always told how good he is and how exceptional he is responds by acting out that praise. The principle is simple: If you lift them up and release them, they will succeed. If you squeeze them harshly, they will die.

This is true in all of life and in all relationships. Our government would do well to take lessons from good parents. Our entire governmental system has become formal, distant, technical, impersonal and demeaning. It has lost the relational touch of the service oriented beginnings we started with. We are killing many Beethoven's.

Some years ago I worked in an Indian Reservation as Construction Manager. I found myself awash with emotions and discoveries as I tried to unravel why the tribe had not built any houses for 20 plus years. I could see no reason for this lack of productive activity. Slowly, I began to put together what was a mosaic of pieces, obvious to see, but not understood by the tribe itself.

The Indian people were not stupid. To the contrary, they were bright, intelligent and capable of many things. There was also a sense of shame and a feeling that they were different and could not compete with the rest of the world. I disagreed. There was nothing keeping this fine people from being part of mainstream America but the sense of dependence they had learned. Almost the entire financial foundations for the tribe's existence consisted of government grants and programs. The people were taken care of and for generations had been given payment for the government's acceptance of guilt for taking their land and injuring their culture. The relationship was one of dependence and demand. The people demanded reparations for the evil perpetrated upon them and government complied, well, sort of. There was never enough money given to raise their level of existence above a certain level, so the people learned to live within the limits of the care given.

One day a young couple came to me for advice. He was a smart young man and I knew instinctively he was destined for honor among his people. His young wife was equally bright and they wanted to explore the possibility of getting one of the new houses we were planning. But, they wanted to be part of the planning process and to shape the house they were hoping to buy to fit their needs and desires. I explained that HUD had limits on the size and expense of the houses it would build for them, so they could not get what they wanted on the reservation. I then asked them why they did not go off reservation and buy what they wanted. They sat there in shock, as though I was nuts. I did not understand that this was, in their world, impossible.

I explained that it was not impossible at all. He had good work skills and work ethic and could easily find employment in any field he wanted. At that time, his construction experience would probably land him a good job in most of the building trades. I explained that if he raised his level of income he could qualify for the house they wanted. Again, they just sat there staring at me. Then they explained this was impossible because they were Indians and they were expected to remain on the reservation and live among their people. The cycle of dependence had conditioned them to the controls of the governmental stipend. They did later find the courage to explore life beyond the limitations of the reservation and seemed happy in their new discovery.

As I was talking to them I illustrated by telling them of my chores as a child. Each of us children had assigned chores and the running of our little family farm was conditional upon our taking care of them. The chickens and rabbits were my responsibility as was the garden. I well remember taking the young chickens and holding them while dad clipped their wing feathers. He explained they could not fly well, like a bird, but they could fly and would get out of the coop if they were not clipped. Then I asked why we did not clip the feathers on the older chickens, and dad explained that once they find out they cannot fly they give up trying and stay forever in the coop.

So it is with the human race. All of us grow up on some sort of reservation - the confines of our life and the expectations others have created for us. If we try to fly out, we get our wings clipped and then, from that point in time we are earthbound - never able to break the bondages of learned dependence and to become the Beethoven we are capable of becoming. Whether that fence is a social context, such as a reservation, or a community, or a church, or a family unit or... It does not matter what the enclosure is, it is the control we learn and that we forever define as the boundaries to our reality.

The wise parent understands this and will encourage the child to incrementally let go of mother's apron strings and walk into the beauty of their potential. But government seems incapable of having that perspective. It is given to fence building and wing clipping. It is regimented, impersonal, confining and given to growing levels of care and the resulting dependency it builds. It is filled with bureaus, whose sole function is to regulate, control and build empires of influence while squashing the life out of the very people it was designed to serve. This ought not to be.

I often wondered if the chicken ever stood at the fence and wondered what life was like on the other side. Then, as I dealt with them over time, I suspected that they had little thought of anything other than the next meal. I wonder yet if the human race is winding down and becoming a blob of empty protoplasm, demeaned by the burden of control and regulations and doomed to never again dream of the next symphony, the next master painting or the next invention that rocks the world. I wonder if we have lost both our dignity and our drive to create and succeed in a world of programs for anything and regulations of everything.

But if not, then what can we do to open the door, tear down the fences, and escape into the bright sunlight of life? How shall we find the freedom that we came to these shores to enjoy and the creativity that it promised?

The answer is simple, but it is also scary. We have to tear down the fence. That is not a cry for lawlessness, for we need and want the government to provide protection from our enemies foreign and domestic. However, we do not need protection from ourselves and our neighbors and regulations against getting up in the morning and taking a shower and flushing the toilet. Alas, waiting for the fences to fall down and the government to get smaller and less intrusive is a mythical illusion that is not substantiated by history. Fences fall when those inside decide to get rid of them. They have to be defined and confronted.

It is the duty of the people, who should hold the power, when they see that the power is now beyond their control, to bring it back into control. We the people are the key to change and until we determine that we will not give away our power nor allow the illegitimate power of others to control us, we will live forever in the chains of tyranny.

It starts with good people running for governmental office and refusing to be corrupted by the power structures they encounter in their rise to responsibility. It happens by refusing to be seduced by the politician who promises to solve our problems and give us what we need. It happens by not allowing our local governments to try to 'cover all the bases' in legislating human activity. It happens by our being aware, being activated, being motivated and refusing to give power to those who become power hungry control freaks.

If we can wake up and understand the nature of power and the abuses that surround us, we can demand accountability to the people for the power given. If we do, then our best days are yet ahead. We can recover our economic equilibrium, find the values we were established on, release creativity and ingenuity, and once again become, the Greatest Nation in history, founded on the American dream of opportunity and resourcefulness.

Beethoven is long gone, but the principle yet remains. The creative genius that resides in every person, from every age, and from every race, is waiting for expression. It only needs the encouragement of the wise parent who will allow the freedom for discovery. There are no limits to what that can mean, unless we continue to clip the wings and regulate the culture into total dependence.

Let's not!

Quotes From Our Founding Fathers (and others!)

Out of adversity comes opportunity. Ben Franklin

"Government's view of the economy could be summed up in a few short phrases: If it moves, tax it. If it keeps moving, regulate it. And if it stops moving, subsidize it" Ronald Reagan

"I, however, place economy among the first and most important republican virtues, and public debt as the greatest of the dangers to be feared." Thomas Jefferson

"Economists are pessimists: they've predicted 8 of the last 3 depressions" Barry Asmus

The economy depends about as much on economists as the weather does on weather forecasters."

"An economy hampered by restrictive tax rates will never produce enough revenue to balance our budget, just as it will never produce enough jobs or enough profits" John Fitzgerald Kennedy

According to the Bank of England the economy is growing too fast so interest rates must rise to counter the supposed inflationary threat. In lay terms, I interpret this to mean that people are working much harder, causing economic growth, and they're in danger of spending their money, which is what the recession-hit shops want them to do. But the Bank and the City seem to think this is wrong, and that if people work harder they should be punished by having their mortgages increased. Harry Enfield

An economist is someone who knows more about money than the people who have it. Anonymous

An economist's guess is liable to be as good as anybody else's. Will Rogers

Ask five economists and you'll get five different explanations? six if one went to Harvard. Edgar R. Fiedler

Commerce changes the fate and genius of nations. Thomas Gray

Genius changes the fate and commerce of nations. David Fritsche
Approximately 80% of our air pollution stems from hydrocarbons released by vegetation, so let's not go overboard in setting and enforcing tough emission standards from man-made sources. Ronald Reagan

Don't be afraid to see what you see. Ronald Reagan

Entrepreneurs and their small enterprises are responsible for almost all the economic growth in the United States. Ronald Reagan

Government always finds a need for whatever money it gets. Ronald Reagan

Government does not solve problems; it subsidizes them. Ronald Reagan

How do you tell a communist? Well, it's someone who reads Marx and Lenin. And how do you tell an anti-Communist? It's someone who understands Marx and Lenin. Ronald Reagan

There are no great limits to growth because there are no limits of human intelligence, imagination, and wonder. Ronald Reagan

There is a very easy way to return from a casino with a small fortune: go there with a large one. Jack Yelton

I am opposed to millionaires, but it would be dangerous to offer me the position. ~Mark Twain

After a visit to the beach, it's hard to believe that we live in a material world. ~Pam Shaw

A bank is a place that will lend you money if you can prove that you don't need it. ~Bob Hope

RESOURCES

http://en.wikipedia.org/wiki/Estates-General_of_1789

http://www.royal.gov.uk/HistoryoftheMonarchy/KingsandQueensoftheUnitedKingdom/TheHanoverians/GeorgeIII.aspx

http://www.al-anon.alateen.org/

http://en.wikipedia.org/wiki/John_Dalberg-Acton,_1st_Baron_Acton

http://en.wikipedia.org/wiki/George_Washington

http://www.thedailybeast.com/newsweek/2010/10/17/how-tea-partiers-get-the-constitution-wrong.html

http://centristnetblog.com/daily/senior-democrat-dingell-obamacare-prepping-to-control-the-people-by-2014/

http://www.lonelyplanet.com/usa/washington-dc/history

http://www.ehow.com/about_5484217_importance-density.html

www.ingramcontent.com/pod-product-compliance
Lightning Source LLC
Chambersburg PA
CBHW070201290526

45789CB00002B/871